Norden: Building a Working Model Victorian Steam Engine

A Workshop Handbook for Model Engineers.

Neil M. Wyatt

Produced in the United Kingdom

First Edition, 2017, second printing with minor revisions 2020.

ISBN: 9781520625188

www.stubmandrel.co.uk

One of the attractions of model engineering is the opportunity to makes a model of unusual prototypes, perhaps something that no-one has tackled before. Supreme examples of this could be the gold-medal recreations of strange Victorian steam vehicles that grace the exhibitions. Some of these were never constructed in full size, despite the hopes of their patent holders! But this does not mean you have to be an elite modeller to enjoy the satisfaction of creating a distinctive model. There are hundreds of small stationary engines to be tracked down, in old engravings, in photographs, in museums and even on scrapheaps. Google Books is a particularly rewarding source of engravings of old steam engines and mechanical devices. Some old engravings have almost every detail in them, but it is possible to make a feasible reconstruction of a model from even the most basic of information. There is no magic formula required, just model engineer's ingenuity and perhaps an ability to 'think in scale'. I would like to recount the story of how I went about recreating a 'lost' steam engine. It all started several years ago when, reading some yellowing post-war issues of Model Engineer, I came across the following letter from Model Engineer Number 2403, Volume 96, p.726, 12 June 1947:

An Old Steam Engine

DEAR SIR,— In the ruins of an old mill at Norden, near Rochdale, there is an old steam engine which has been left rotting away with five others, and a Lancashire Boiler.

The bed of this engine was like a table, cast with the top and legs in one piece and bolted down to a cast iron bedplate, which in turn is bolted to a slab of concrete. The height of the table is 4 ft. 6 in., and the top of the table measures 2 ft. 4 1/2 in. by 1 ft. 5 1/2 in.

The flywheel is 4 ft. 3 in. diameter by 5 in. face. There are six curved spokes of + section.

The cylinder is bolted direct to the bedplate by its bottom flange. The bore is approximately 9 in. and the stroke is 13 in.

The crosshead is of the alligator-type and runs between locomotive-type slide bars, which are 2 ft. 3 1/2 in. long by 2 1/4 in. wide.

The connecting rod is bellied and has strap and cotter big- and little-ends. The centres of the connecting rod are 2 ft. 1 in.

The crankshaft is 2 1/2 in. diameter and rests in two bearings, one at each end of the table ; the single crank web is balanced.

The governor has two 5 in. diameter balls and was driven direct off the crankshaft by bevel gears to the tops of the governor spindle. I have no idea of the age, origin, speed or working pressure of this engine, but probably some reader could throw some light on the matter.

Yours faithfully,

Shaw, Lancs.   S. Lees.

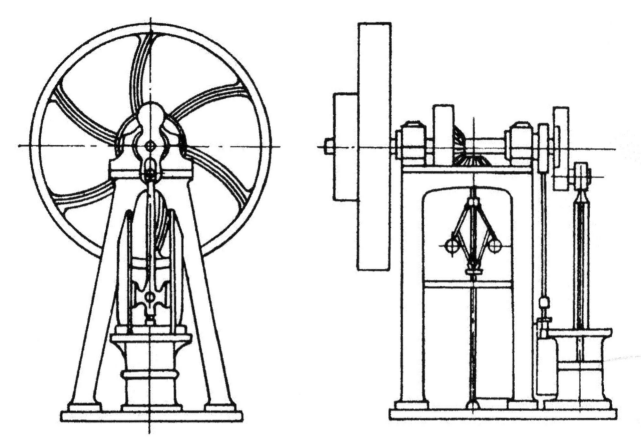

Elevtions of the old steam engine in Lancashire

A tiny sketch, reproduced here larger than original size (Fig. 2) accompanied the letter. I had been considering making a scale model of an 'interesting' prototype for some time. Despite its apparent simplicity, the sketched engine was characterful and immediately appealing – it is clear why it attracted Mr Lees notice. The 'bed like a table', distinctive flywheel and the arrangement of cylinder and slide bars all looked like presenting worthwhile challenges. None of these challenges was too difficult to overcome, and the end result was an unusual and rewarding model (Photos 1,2).

The model is based solely on Mr Lees drawing and description. In all cases I followed the dimensions in the letter exactly. Except where the sketch is obviously simplified, I followed it as closely as is practicable. I don't claim perfection, and there are a few areas where constructors might improve on my interpretation.

One of my first tasks was to see just what information I really had about the engine. What did Mr Lees letter and drawing tell me? What could be extrapolated from them? Finally, what was left out? It was quite surprising how much information can be gleaned from these sparse sources. The engine is from an old mill at Norden near Rochdale. The only similar engines I found picture of were small colliery winding engines, but this is not a colliery engine. A mill engine would not have been reversible, and would need to run at a controlled speed, consistent with both the governor and lack of reversing gear. The drawing indicates two pulleys that would have allowed the engine to drive line shafting in the mill. It was 'old' in the 1940s, by which time the mill itself had fallen into ruin. The design seems typical of the mid-late1800s to my relatively untrained eye. It was one of six, possibly not the same as any of the others, and probably the most remarkable (else why pick this one to report on?). There was one Lancashire boiler; presumably powering several if not all of the engines. I like to think that this old-fashioned engine was an early experiment in steam power by the mill that found a niche alongside later, larger and more powerful engines. Perhaps it was a useful standby, a source of auxiliary power or maybe it ran some small process or activity over a long and useful life?

The letter and sketch conflict in just two places – the dimensions of the governor balls and the face of the flywheel are not drawn to the specified dimensions. In both cases I followed the letter. The most obvious effect of this is that the governor balls on the model look a lot larger than those drawn in the sketch. Three-inch balls as per the sketch might be rather small for a Watt Governor - another engine of similar date that I have an accurate engraving of appears to have 4" balls. This suggested to me that the drawing was probably made to the main dimensions, perhaps guided by some quick sketches, then finished from memory. When scaling from the drawing, I assumed that sizes are approximate, and assumed the full size would generally be built more or less to inches or significant fractions of an inch. As well as information of which I could be confident, there was a lot I could work out by extrapolation. Unlike Donald Rumsfeld, I chose not to lose sleep worrying about the unknown unknowns. It is clear that the relative proportions of the various parts of any stationary steam engine do not vary greatly, so a policy of copying parts from similar-sized engines is unlikely to result in disproportionate results. As far as I have been able, for all (known) unknown details I have tried to follow my understanding of nineteenth century practice. The one notable (but hidden) exception has been using o-rings instead of loose packing for the glands and piston.

A few years after completing the engine, I discovered the existence of some a-frame engines by John Chadwick. These bear such a strong family resemblance the original may have been a Chadwick engine, although I think the Norden engine is rather older, and Mr Lees did not record the maker's name cast into the frame. There are differences in the Chadwick engine from with both my model and Mr Lees' drawing – be these errors or just because it is a different model. But it confirms one thing - the large size of the governor balls is appropriate!

I decided early on to work to a scale of 1:12. This would be well within the capacity of my equipment, whilst keeping calculations simple. It would produce a model of reasonably compact proportions whilst being large enough for scale sized fixings to be used (Fig. 1). The flywheel is 4 1/4" diameter, so even a 2 1/2" centre height lathe could be used to make this model. Working drawings were prepared using Corel Draw, mainly to check clearances and to 'share out' available space between different components. I did not produce fully dimensioned or detailed drawings, so the drawings accompanying this series have been drawn from the model. I have a personal preference for imperial dimensions for models of 'imperial' originals, so almost all measurement was in inches (which seem to be doing just as well in the real world as they were when ME writers were predicting their imminent extinction over a quarter century ago). This is why the drawings are dimensioned in inches. I have given no indications of types of fit; model engineers don't make parts to be interchangeable and have the wits to understand the difference needed between a shaft running in its bearing and a flywheel fixed on its shaft. Some dimensions will need to be checked as you go, especially to allow for variations in fabricating the table.

I produced my own patterns and had castings made for key components and tried to avoid buying in anything other than fixings. On the whole, I achieved my aim, which makes an unusual model of a unique engine. Although there were some interesting puzzles along the way I didn't encounter any problems that would stop any model engineer from doing the same. Whilst I can't promise anyone a gold medal, I am happy to assert that any reader of this magazine who has already built a simple steam engine, is capable of building the engine.

To summarise what I did myself: all of the castings (base, cylinder, pulleys, flywheel) are from my own patterns. The patterns for the flywheel and the two smaller pulleys were turned and milled from solid disks of aluminium alloy. The pattern for the base was fabricated from basswood (lime) and birch plywood. That for the cylinder comprised several materials, including wood, aluminium and acrylic sheet.

Some other details of the model are that castings were obtained for the steam chest and its cover and the cylinder top cover, but the patterns were undersized and the parts machined from the solid instead. I have since remade the patterns for these parts. The table is not a casting; a pattern was prepared, but rejected as too complex to cast at this scale.

For those wishing to build this model, I have lodged the patterns with longstanding supplier Blackgates Engineering ([1] http://www.blackgates.co.uk/), who can also supply full sets of drawings.

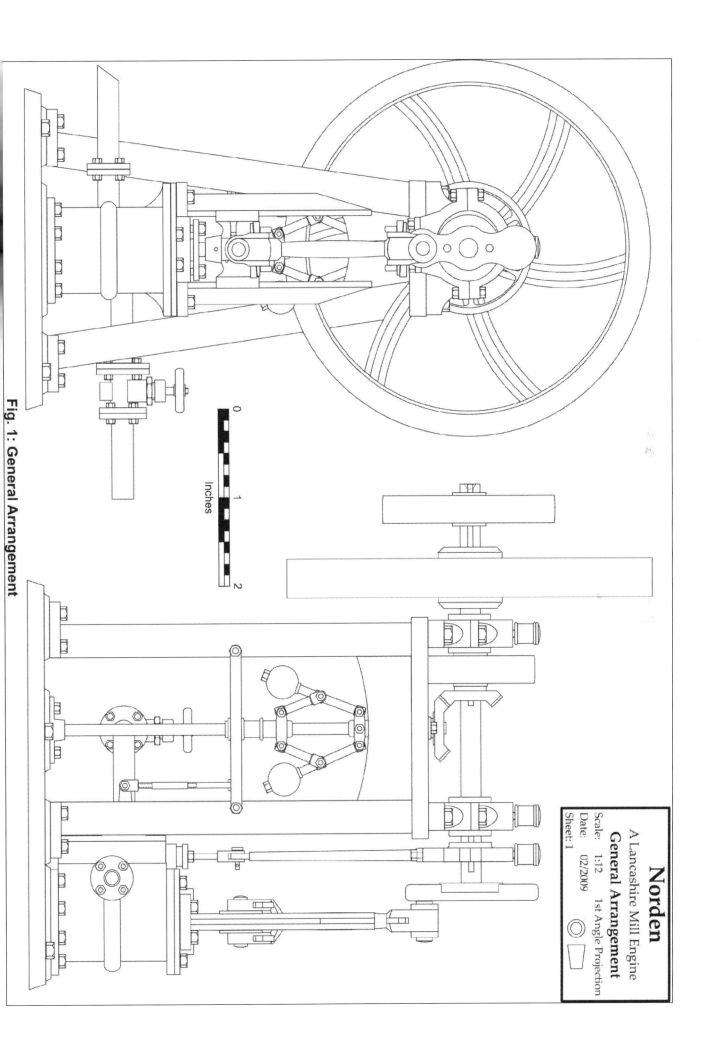

Fig. 1 : General Arrangement

0
Inches
1
2

Norden
A Lancashire Mill Engine
General Arrangement

Scale: 1:12   1st Angle Projection
Date: 02/2009
Sheet: 1

The governor spindle runs in brass bushes and operates a butterfly valve on the front of the steamchest. It works, but is not very effective – speed control is best left to careful adjustment of the steam stop valve. All the parts assembled to the crankshaft are held in place solely by cotters and wedges, and the piston rod bearings have three sets of wedges and cotters. I machined the bevel gears with my own cutter made using the methods described by Ivan Law. I used brass gears rather than cast iron ones, though brass were used on some prototypical gears of this size (9" diameter) cast iron would be more likely.

Aside from production of the patterns, the model took about five months of spare time to construct. The main machine tools used were a much-modified Clarke CL300M lathe, a pillar drill and an ARC X2 mill. My bandsaw also played its part.

The finished engine runs smoothly and very quietly on air at less than 1.4psi (Measured on a genuine and rather fine 19th century Compound Gauge by Bourdon of Paris, reading +/- 4psi) at a steady 70 rpm, and with care can be persuaded to run slower than this.

This is a detailed model and perhaps not ideal for an absolute beginner, so rather than describing every machining operation in detail, I will illustrate how I interpreted the relatively sparse information on Norden, and how I filled in the gaps. I will give guidance on the more difficult and unusual machining operations, including some lessons I learnt along the way. Next time I shall start by describing the table and base for the engine.

Neil Wyatt

Branston, Staffordshire, 2016

Postscript

I have since discovered, or been guided to, a small number of Chadwick engines., notably at the Northern Mill Engine Society and the Manchester Museum of Science and Industry. These engines all appear different to Mr Lee's description of Norden, which may represent one of Chadwick's earlier engines. All of these engines have three features not seen in Norden – the A-frame is bolted down inside the angle of the legs and the guide bars are braced to the A-frame, finally, the 'alligator-crosshead' is hollow and the connecting rod has a single eye, instead of a fork as I have modelled it. You may wish to incorporate these features in your model, as I suspect that this would have been the arrangement on the original prototype of Norden..

Chapter 2: The Table and Bedplate

"The bed of this engine was like a table, cast with the top and legs in one piece and bolted down to a cast iron bedplate, which in turn is bolted to a slab of concrete. The height of the table is 4 ft. 6 in., and the top of the table measures 2 ft. 4 1/2 in. by 1 ft. 5 1/2 in. ... The cylinder is bolted direct to the bedplate by its bottom flange."

My starting point for the engine was to make patterns for various parts, but in order to follow a logical 'route' around the engine I'd like to start with the table and bedplate. After all, these are what give the engine its character. Mr Lees gave us enough detail to have a fair idea of the construction of the table (fig. 10), though his drawing shows the bedplate as just a plain flat plate. Finishing such a large area would have been a great deal of work and it is more likely that the bedplate would have had raised pads for these items. These pads would have been machined or, perhaps more likely, hand finished.

The drawing shows a bottom flange for the cylinder that is too narrow to allow the fixing of nuts over any studs from below. There are two possible solutions – a wider flange for the lower end of the cylinder or a square flange. I decided on a square flange with six studs holding down the cylinder. If you prefer you can round off the flange to your own taste.

The drawing also shows the base of the legs with insufficient flanges for fixing to the base. The answer cannot be one big stud inside the angle of the legs, as this would make the base impossible to cast in one piece. I assumed that the legs join the pads offset towards the inner corner, as the table is cast in one piece (quite an achievement!) From the drawings I estimated the scale size of the pads to be 5/8" square.

The drawing also shows a bearing at the base of the governor spindle, so I included a small pad for attaching a bearing.

So the first part is the bedplate (fig. 3). The engine bedplate pattern (photo 3) was made from 3mm basswood, with strips glued to the underside. The pads were cut from 2mm litely and faired in with filler. The resulting casting was a good one, with a little flash on two sides. I ground off the bulk of the flash, and tidied up the sides of the casting with a file. I was able to hold it gently by the edges in a milling vice to take a gentle skim across the six pads. Having recently spent several evenings scraping the column bracket of my mill to get it both vertical and rigid, I was rewarded with a very good surface. The cylinder base was finished by gentle polishing with fine abrasive paper supported on a glass sheet.

Inverted, the base would now lie true on the bed of the mill. I clamped it down with three clamps (well two at a time so that I could reach all parts of the casting) to take a skim off the underside to make it truly parallel with the top of the pads. Drilling the baseplate is best left until the various mating parts have been completed, in order to be sure that everything lines up, especially the cylinder mounting studs.

If you wish to fabricate the base, rather than use the casting, I suggest you make pads from 1/16" brass or steel sheet and soft solder them in place on a sheet of 3/16" or 4mm steel.

I had originally set out to produce a pattern for a cast table. Once complete it was apparent that there was no way I could reasonably ask anyone to transform this pattern into a usable casting (photo 4). I tried breaking the casting down into three components, and decided that assembling these would be more difficult than fabricating the entire table.

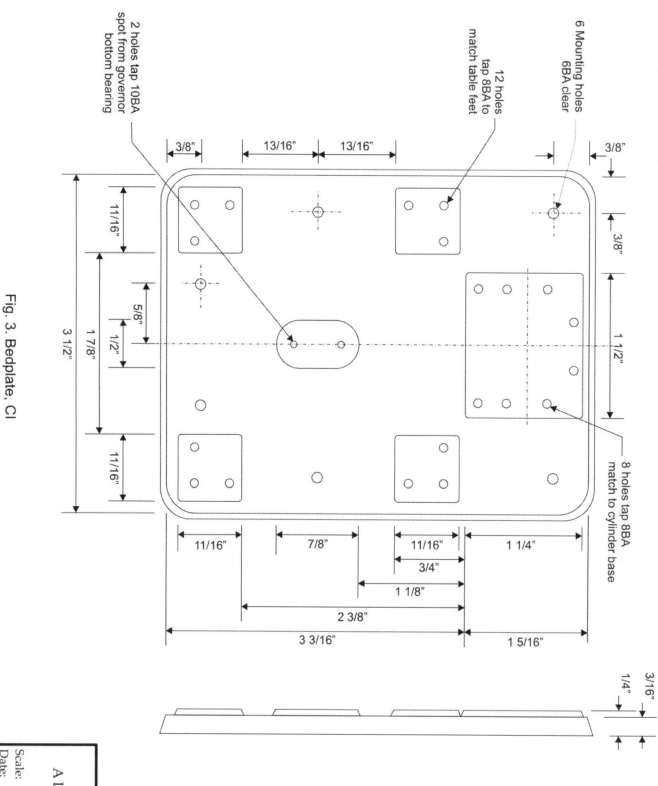

Fig. 3. Bedplate, CI

2 holes tap 10BA
spot from governor
bottom bearing

12 holes
tap 8BA to
match table feet

6 Mounting holes
6BA clear

8 holes tap 8BA
match to cylinder base

3/8"
13/16"
13/16"
3/8"

11/16"
5/8"
1/2"
1 7/8"
3 1/2"
11/16"

3/8"
1 1/2"

11/16"
7/8"
11/16"
1 1/4"
3/4"
1 1/8"
2 3/8"
3 3/16"
1 5/16"

3/16"
1/4"

Norden
A Lancashire Mill Engine
Bedplate
Scale: 1:12
Date: 02/2009
Sheet: 3
1st Angle Projection

The fabricated table (Figs. 4-8) is made of the top, four legs, four filler pieces between the legs and four 'feet' or flanges at the base of each leg and, optionally, 20 pieces of brass boiler banding. Mr Lees was adamant the bed was cast in one piece, yet the Chadwick engine I found pictured had the table as two end castings held together by several hefty pieces riveted between them – evidence they are not the same engines, even if related.

I started by searching for a suitable source of angle to make the legs of the table. I was carrying out a workshop spring clean and re-discovered some rough, ratty black steel angle from some old shelving. A nominal 1" on each side and 1/8" thick, it had a slightly rounded profile inside and outside on the corner. After cutting roughly to length, I used a slitting saw in the mill to cut out the 3/8" corner of each piece of angle. On a first attempt with a thin saw the slot wandered, but a thicker (1/16") saw gave an excellent result. I used my bandsaw to cut the ends to length an at the appropriate angle. Only then did I treat each leg with paint stripper and discover how rough the finish on the angle was! Time for some draw filing…

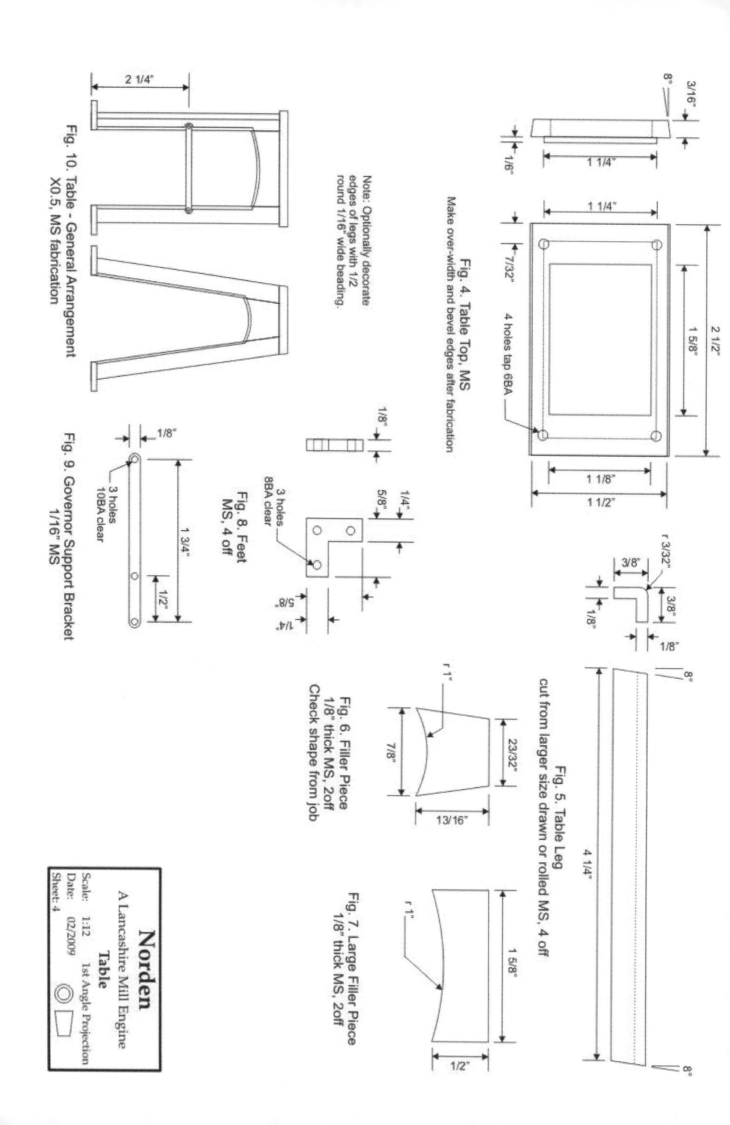

Fig. 4. Table Top, MS

Make over-width and bevel edges after fabrication

3/16"
8°
1/6"
1 1/4"

2 1/2"
1 5/8"
1 1/4"
7/32"
4 holes tap 6BA
1 1/8"
1 1/2"

Fig. 5. Table Leg
cut from larger size drawn or rolled MS, 4 off

r 3/32"
3/8"
3/8"
1/8"
1/8"
8°
4 1/4"
1 5/8"
8°

Note: Optionally decorate
edges of legs with 1/2
round 1/16" wide beading.

Fig. 8. Feet
MS, 4 off

1/8"
1/4"
5/8"
5/8"
1/4"

3 holes
8BA clear

Fig. 6. Filler Piece
1/8" thick MS, 2off
Check shape from job

r 1"
7/8"
23/32"
13/16"

Fig. 7. Large Filler Piece
1/8" thick MS, 2off

r 1"
1/2"

Fig. 9. Governor Support Bracket
1/16" MS

1/8"
1 3/4"
1/2"

3 holes
10BA clear

Fig. 10. Table - General Arrangement
X0.5, MS fabrication

2 1/4"

Norden
A Lancashire Mill Engine
Table

Scale: 1:12   1st Angle Projection
Date: 02/2009
Sheet: 4

The top could have been easily cut from some 3/16" sheet – but I only had 1/8" and this was too thin to allow decent flanges to be milled to secure the other parts to. Fortunately I had a larger block, but 1" thick. Three cheers for electric bandsaws – I could never have made a neat job of cutting off a slice by hand. The resulting piece was slightly tapered, and a little thick, so I brought it parallel in the mill, also truing up the two ends. I marked out the centre hole using a height gauge on the surface plate, then chain drilled out most of the centre portion. Then mill and file to tidy up the hole, and to produce a rebate around the bottom of the base against which the legs and filler pieces could locate.

Before making the filler pieces to fit, I decided to get the legs jigged into position. I discovered that this was not going to be an easy task. I will describe the merry dance I went through to assemble the table from this uneven material. I strongly suggest you use bright drawn steel angle, which will be easy to clamp allowing you to avoid all these shenanigans.

Because the angle for the legs was rounded off, inside and out, I could not clamp it securely. It kept twisting and the rounded inside corners also meant I could not get a positive location from rebate underneath the table. To cut a long story short I used chipboard and four square wooden strips to make a frame to locate the four legs. I cut an angled block of 1 1/4" plywood to fit inside the legs and, after a little adjustment, it was possible to place this in the frame and wedge one leg into each corner between block and frame. Two pieces of softwood glued across the top of the block served to keep the legs at the correct spacing and with a little packing and some rubber bands it the top would neatly sit on top of the whole assembly. Unfortunately the rounded material still prevented me from securely clamping everything. I invested in a bag of quick setting mortar. I made up a small quantity, rather stiffer than normal, and liberally worked it in and around the whole base of the assembly. While its set and dried I scribed the angles for the tapered filler pieces onto 1/8" steel strip and got on with cutting and filling them to shape (photo 5).

Making the filler pieces was easy enough – I superglued two blanks together while filing out the curve on the underside, to make sure they matched. To hold them in place for silver soldering I settled upon making a temporary cross piece with two notches cut and filed so the inside dimension was exactly right to space the two pieces. The ends were sawn to make tabs thin enough to be bent over with a small hammer and grip the pieces firmly in place. I decided that the two long, thin filler pieces could be added later, using soft solder.

By the next day I was comfortable that the mortar was well and truly set and reasonably dry. I checked the fit of all parts and put the table, all coated in flux, upside down on an insulating block. I didn't bake the mortar as it is porous and I was optimistic that any steam generated by indirect heat would escape without cracking it.

I used a medium sized gas blowlamp and I was able to complete the job in one go. The softwood blocks had charred by the end, but the jig held without complaint, even when gently hosed with cold water. Once cool, I was wondering how to get the table out of the mortar. By accident I dropped the whole assembly a few inches onto a wooden pallet, the mortar split asunder and the job dropped out clean as a whistle!

I cleaned off the flux using sulphamic acid (which is sold as limescale remover). This is a really effective pickle that doesn't have the nasty side effects of sulphuric acid, though you should still wash everything with plenty of clean water.

Again, I suggest you use cold drawn steel angle to make the legs. This is virtually square, inside and out, though it may need a little truing up. Even so, it should easy to jig together the table simply by clamping the base of legs to a suitably shaped piece of wood. Another idea is to fit a few small screws to help hold everything together – they can be sawn off and filed flush later.

The next task was attaching the 'feet' or flanges to the base of the legs. These were little L-shapes made by milling out a corner from 5/8" square bar, then taking 1/8" slices in the bandsaw. Silver soldering these was straightforward, the only points being that I used plenty of solder to ensure a good fillet, and a little wooden stick to hold the feet in position.

Once I had cleaned the table up again, I saw that a little judicious filing would be needed to bring the filler pieces flush with the legs (photo 6). The spacer piece had also become securely soldered in place. I cut the centre portion of the spacer out using a rotary tool with a cut-off wheel, then tidied things up by filing.

The two final filler pieces were straightforward to make, though soft soldering them in position was tricky. I could not get the solder to 'run' into the joint. In the end I tinned the mating surfaces and heated everything until the solder ran and then assemble the parts into place with pliers. Luckily the table is big enough that it was possible to do one side at a time without the first side collapsing.

The finish on the cold-drawn angle was pretty rough (think corduroy), but after some judicious draw-filing and the application of a skim of filler it looked more like a scaled down casting. The final touch, added after the holes for the governor support bars (fig. 9) were drilled, was 1/16" half-round boiler banding around the insides of the legs. I could have soft soldered these on, but chose to use Loctite. One side of each mitre joint was cut in place with a razor saw, then a loose piece was filed to fit. Curving the banding around the arched tops was done first, and accomplished with the careful use of pliers and a little swearing. The tight curves around the fixing holes were made easier with a simple jig. I turned a narrow groove 1/16" deep in a suitable steel bar, and wrapped an annealed piece of banding sideways into the groove. It was left a little twisted, but now be easily flattened to shape. The radius was finished against a spigot on the jig. I cut and filed the four curved pieces to match each other, before fixing them. At this point I felt that the table started to 'look the business' (photo 7). I was ready to fix it to the bedplate.

'Bolted down' is an interesting comment by Mr Lees. One would expect the table and cylinder to be held in place by studs in the bedplate, but is it possible that bolts were used to assemble these parts? The cylinder and table could be edged into position and the bolts dropped down the holes. Plausible though this is I suspect not, and that 'bolted' is being used in its lay sense. I decided the obvious solution was studs. I used 8BA as a reasonable facsimile for 1" full size, with 'one size smaller' nuts to avoid a clumsy appearance. The Chadwick engine uses a single stud inside each 'foot' of the table, a near impossible arrangement for an engine with the table is cast in one piece. If you wish to do this, it's easy enough to arrange if you shorten the legs by 1/8" and use squares instead of L-shapes for the mounting flanges.

Now the engine has a skeleton, I will take the rest of the engine 'from the top' starting with its characteristic flywheel.

Chapter 3: Flywheel

The engine's elegant flywheel was 4' 3" diameter by 5" face. The drawing shows the flywheel with a very thin, broad rim – this is most unlikely, especially for a mill engine, a use requiring a steady drive speed. I assumed the quoted face width was accurate and that the depth of the flywheel rim would be approximately the same. If you wish to make the rim thinner, it is easy to do so, but the engine may not run as smoothly at low speeds.

The spokes are curved and of a cross shaped section, one of the most distinctive features of the engine (fig. 11). I decided that I would make a pattern for the flywheel and have a casting made. Making the pattern was a big challenge, having six curved spokes, cross-shaped in section. The options were to mill a pattern from aluminium alloy, or build up a pattern from thin wooden laminations.

Creating a scale drawing of the flywheel it was soon apparent that the basic geometry to generate the spokes was fairly straightforward. I decided to make the flywheel as a pattern in aluminium alloy, and have a casting made for two reasons. Firstly, the pattern would be available to make further copies in the future and secondly, working in a softer material would be quicker and easier on cutters, equipment and nerves.

I started with a large alloy blank. To allow me to centre, remove and replace it, I turned up a simple stepped plug for my rotary table and faceplate, with a spigot that was a tight fit in a 1/4" hole drilled in the centre of the blank. The diameter of the flywheel made attaching the blank to the 7" faceplate difficult. I tapped two M3 holes just inside the rim to allow me to screw the blank to the faceplate. The next operation was to skim the two sides of the blank so they were parallel.

I then moved the blank to the rotary table and drilled six 1/8" holes at 60° (10-turn) intervals as reference points where the spokes joined the rim. I then milled a recess to create a web from which to mill the spokes, including leaving a small step inside the rim. To mill out the spokes I first made another plug gauge, this one with a 1/8" spigot to fit in the six holes. For these operations the blank was held with an ordinary clamp.

Milling the spokes was then slow, but straightforward. I used the next hole along to set the cutter at the correct radius for the outside arc of the first spoke. By turning the table I then cut a slot from the hole to the hub (leaving a little metal around the hole so it could be used again when the wheel was turned over). I then moved the table along its x-axis by 2mm to cut the outer step in the spoke. With suitable further feed this was followed by the inner step and then the inside arc of the spoke. At least, that's how I would do it now. The arms of the flywheel are drawn as quite robust, in comparison to the rim of the flywheel. Allowing for variation in the drawing and line thickness it is probable that the spokes were more delicate. The first time I took 1/8" steps and made spokes 3/8" wide. These looked really clumsy in three dimensions, and I had to do virtually the whole process again to reduce them in height and width.

One problem I had not anticipated was the bright, shiny finish of the cut metal. Combined with the safety goggles, at times it was difficult to get an accurate understanding of how the shape of the spokes was emerging. The regular application of a vacuum cleaner nozzle helped. In fact, if the holes are in the right place, the spokes automatically come out right, all I had to do is watch the progress of the cutter and work the slots until the cutter just contacted the hub or rim.

The next stage was to turn the blank over and machine the other side of the spokes (remembering that they curve the opposite way on the other side!) I had not made the side arcs deep enough to cut right through, so the first stage for each spoke was an exploratory hole to find the edge of the buried spoke. It was then an easy job to cut the two arcs that defined the spoke rib. I also machined off the locating holes as I went around.

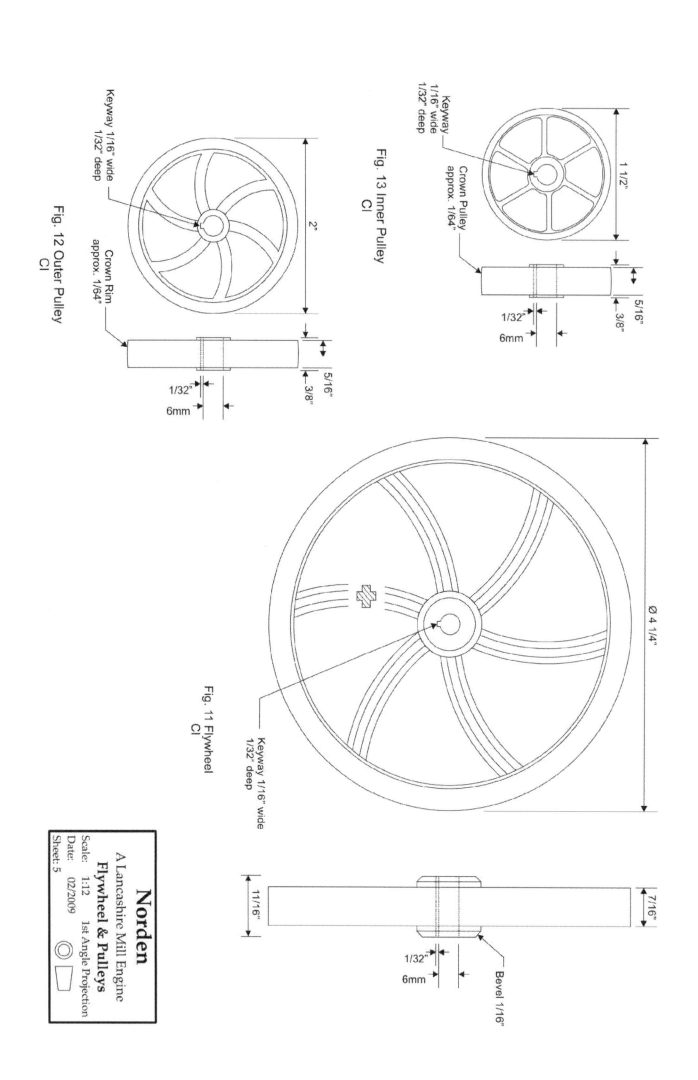

Fig. 13 Inner Pulley
CI

Keyway 1/16" wide
1/32" deep

Crown Pulley
approx. 1/64"

1 1/2"

5/16"
3/8"
1/32"
6mm

Fig. 12 Outer Pulley
CI

Keyway 1/16" wide
1/32" deep

Crown Rim
approx. 1/64"

2"

5/16"
3/8"
1/32"
6mm

Fig. 11 Flywheel
CI

Keyway 1/16" wide
1/32" deep

Ø 4 1/4"

11/16"

7/16"

1/32"
6mm

Bevel 1/16"

Norden
A Lancashire Mill Engine
Flywheel & Pulleys

Scale: 1:12
Date: 02/2009
Sheet: 5

1st Angle Projection

The final milling task was to re-centre the blank using the plug, and carefully mill along the inside of the rim and outside of the hub. Collecting the little 'Star-Trek symbols' as they fell off was quite rewarding, but not as rewarding as seeing the six finished spokes, even if they did have a few minor defects that I patched up later. All the milling of the spokes was carried out with a single 1/8" FC3 cutter. The heavier removal of material for profiling was done with an 11.5mm slot drill and a 1/2" end mill.

The next job was to put the faceplate back onto the lathe and thin down the rim of the flywheel (leaving a machining allowance). I also put a 1° taper on the hub and the outside of the flywheel, but assumed that the depth of most of the surfaces was small enough not to need significant draft.

I did have a few errors in centring the blank, of the order of 0.2mm. This is not significant, as the casting will probably have errors as big as this, but it did mean that there was some hand filing and fettling to be done on the inside of the rim. After breaking all the sharp edges with needle files, I filled the few spots where the mill had run over.

Unmentioned in Mr Lees' letter are two drive pulleys shown in the drawing, one outside the flywheel and a smaller one adjacent to the crankshaft bevel gear (figs 12,13). The small pulley scales as 18" diameter by 4" face. The large pulley scales as 24" diameter, and is drawn as about 4" face, but having no space between it and the flywheel. It would have needed a working space so the belt would not have fouled the flywheel. The crankshaft needed to be raised by about 1/8" relative to the drawing, otherwise the small inner pulley fouls the table and has no space for a belt to be fitted. Both pulleys would be slightly crowned as they would have driven flat belts. They would probably have had quite thin rims as the original sketch shows for the smaller pulley. Pulleys of these diameters would almost certainly have been spoked. I have assumed the larger pulley had curved spokes, and the smaller pulley had straight ones.

A very similar, but simpler procedure was followed to make patterns for three smaller pulley wheels, one with simple curved spokes and the two others with straight spokes. One of the straight spoked pulleys went to another model. I think it is fair to say that the area of getting castings made from your own patterns is one in which the model engineers of today are far less well served than those of yesteryear. I have made some minor imporvements to the patterns – mostly filleting inside corners and adding some more draft, which should further improve the quality of castings made from them. The patterns are with Blackgates Engineering, who will be able to supply sets of castings for the model.

The flywheel and pulley castings will require a certain amount of fettling (photo 9,10). My original castings had some irregularities on the spokes, where moulding sand had caught in the spokes. I have added small fillets to the inner angles of the spokes on the pattern, which should reduce this problem. If cast iron is chosen, the spokes may cool rapidly and be hard – this cannot really be avoided with such small sections. I used diamond burrs in a mini-drill and diamond files, and it was not a particularly long task to tidy up the spokes of all three wheels.

Once the 'as cast' surfaces were sorted out, turning the rims (photos 11, 12) was a straighforward exercise, as was drilling and reaming their bores. Make sure that you turn the rim of the flywheel and bore it at the same setting. Alternatively mount each wheel on a tight fitting mandrel for a final skim over the edges of the rim. The outer rim of the pulleys should be slightly convex. This is done most conveniently with a file, but make sure the file has a secure handle and use extra care to keep well clear of the chuck.

The bore of the wheels was too small to use my 'Stan Bray' slotting tool for the fixing wedges. Instead I made a guide bush to allow me to make a suitable slot with a needle file. This is just a 'top hat' of hardened silver steel, with a 1/16" slot in it, that is clamped in the bore of the wheel (photo 13). This acts as a filing guide, guaranteeing perfectly aligned slots with minimum fuss.

The natural place to proceed from here is, of course, the crankshaft, so that is what I will look at next.

Chapter 4: Crankshaft

The crankshaft is 2 1/2 in. diameter and rests in two bearings, one at each end of the table ; the single crank web is balanced.

The crankshaft is 2 1/2" diameter and has bearings at each end of the table with a balanced crank web. The crankpin is large, drawn the same diameter as the crankshaft. The crankshaft appears nice and simple, however, inspection of the drawings of the crank web show that this appears to be fixed to a circular flange on the end of the shaft, rather than being integral to it.

The diameter of 2 1/2" scales to 0.208" or 5.28mm - not a convenient stock size. It is rather less than the 1/4" one might expect on a model this size, and perhaps a little flimsy for a working model; 6mm is a suitable compromise (fig. 14), but as I had no 6mm bar, I turned down the shaft from 1/4" stock. I started by centring one end of a slightly over-length bar, then silver soldered a slice of 7/8" bar on the other end. Holding the shaft in the three-jaw chuck, I turned it down to create the flange, not quite finishing it to final diameter and drilled a centre in the disc. With the bar in the three-jaw chuck and a live centre supporting the other end I turned the length of the crankshaft. I was decidedly chuffed to get a result that was no more than a thou out over a 6" length. Finally, I reversed the crankshaft and finished the crank disk. If you want to avoid turning the crankshaft, just use 6mm bar and use high-strength retainer to fix the disk in place.

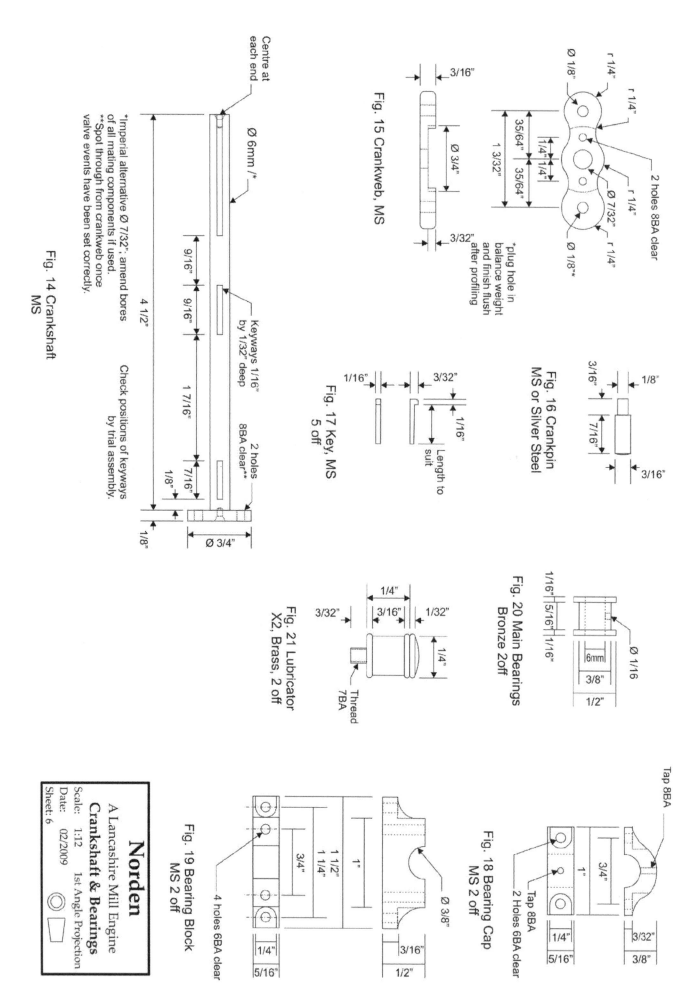

Fig. 14 Crankshaft MS

Centre at each end

Ø 6mm /*

*Imperial alternative Ø 7/32"; amend bores of all mating components if used.
**Spot through from crankweb once valve events have been set correctly.

Check positions of keyways by trial assembly.

4 1/2"

9/16"

9/16"

1 7/16"

7/16"

1/8"

Keyways 1/16" by 1/32" deep

2 holes 8BA clear**

Ø 3/4"

Fig. 15 Crankweb, MS

3/16"

Ø 3/4"

3/32"

Ø 1/8"

r 1/4"

r 1/4"

35/64"

1/4" 1/4"

35/64"

1 3/32"

Ø 7/32"

r 1/4"

Ø 1/8"**

r 1/4"

2 holes 8BA clear

*plug hole in balance weight and finish flush after profiling

Fig. 16 Crankpin MS or Silver Steel

3/16"

1/8"

7/16"

3/16"

Fig. 17 Key, MS 5 off

1/16"

3/32"

1/16"

Length to suit

Fig. 20 Main Bearings Bronze 2off

1/16"

5/16"

1/16"

Ø 1/16

6mm

3/8"

1/2"

Fig. 21 Lubricator X2, Brass, 2 off

3/32"

1/4"

3/16"

1/32"

1/4"

Thread 7BA

Fig. 18 Bearing Cap MS 2 off

Tap 8BA

Tap 8BA

2 Holes 6BA clear

1"

3/4"

1/4"

5/16"

3/32"

3/8"

Fig. 19 Bearing Block MS 2 off

4 holes 6BA clear

1 1/2"

1 1/4"

3/4"

1"

Ø 3/8"

1/4"

5/16"

3/16"

1/2"

Norden
A Lancashire Mill Engine
Crankshaft & Bearings

Scale: 1:12   1st Angle Projection
Date: 02/2009
Sheet: 6

There are several keyways in the crankshaft – I made them all the same section: 1/16" wide by 1/32" deep. I cut them with the edge of a narrow keyway cutter, rather than an end mill – a simple tool made from silver steel with hand-filed teeth. This gave a more accurate width and a more authentic shape to the ends of the keyways. In order the keyed parts are the eccentric, the governor bevel gear, the inner pulley, the flywheel and the outer pulley (photo 14). The keys are filed up from 1/16" thick mild steel (fig. 17). A small vice with 'sharp' edged jaws is very useful for holding such small parts. One disadvantage of using keys is that, if they don't fit perfectly, they can allow the flywheel to wobble. If you can't get a perfect fit, help them out with a little retainer on final assembly.

The crankweb was marked out with three carefully spaced punch marks on a piece of steel plate (fig. 15). Using a wobbler the centre mark was lined up below the mill and a 6mm hole drilled right through. This was then opened up half way through, using a boring head, to a close push fit on the crankshaft flange (photo 15). Both these operations could be done in the lathe, holding the work in a 4-jaw chuck.

A hole was drilled and reamed 3/16" for the crankpin and one 3/16" drilled at the centre of the 'counterweight'. Four 1/2" and two 3/8" filing buttons were made from silver steel, drilled to match the appropriate holes, and hardened but not tempered. These were fixed in place using suitable screws, so that the web could be filed to shape (photo 16). After cutting away excess stock, I used the back of a half-round file to produce the concavities between each circular portion. An ordinary flat file brought the convex curves to size, before finishing with smooth needle files. The hole in the 'counterweight' was filled with chemical metal, as I had originally planned that this part would be painted and the filler would not be visible.

On looking at photographs of nineteenth century engines I saw that many had crankwebs that were elegantly rounded and well finished. Inspired, I went onto the attack with half-round and warding needle files. I then dug out some of those accessories that come with mini-drill kits – starting with a small sanding drum which produced a very fine grained finish. This was followed by a felt drum and polishing compound to get a mirror finish. So far so good, but the chemical metal stood out a mile! I chipped out the filler and turned up a mild steel plug to an interference fit in the hole. After some careful attention with a precision press tool (lump hammer!) the hole was filled. A little more filing, sanding and polishing was needed to get a near 'invisible mend'. I hope the result looks much like the crank webs of some preserved engines, and is not too brightly finished to be out of keeping with the rest of the engine (photo 17).

The crankpin was a simple job (fig.16), but care should be taken to ensure it is truly parallel with the crankshaft. The final step was fitting the crankweb to the crankshaft. As mentioned earlier, the drawing suggests the crankshaft has a disc on one end to which the web is attached. One advantage of this is that I was able to key the eccentric to the crankshaft, and then set the crank to set the valve. Naturally, you will only be able to do this once you have completed the cylinder, steam chest and valve gear!

It took many tries to be 100% satisfied with the valve setting, as I was aiming for smooth low speed running, which meant minimal advance. I used superglue to temporarily fix the crank in place, and once I was satisfied with its position I spotted two holes through the crank through the web on the crankshaft. Into these I fitted two 8BA screws, with their heads turned down to resemble rivets. I would be pleased to hear from any reader who knows just how the real crankshaft might have been built up. I will give more advice on running in and setting up the engine at the end of this series.

The drawing shows the crankshaft bearings in elegantly shaped end housings. Slightly thicker lines on the drawing indicate the bearings are split horizontally (photo 18). Making these bearing blocks was a pleasant task, each being milled from solid bar (figs. 18, 19). The central bore was made with the two parts of each block bolted together, before any detailed shaping was done. The concave curves were made using bull-nosed end mill, but the convex curve on top of each block was filed by hand.

To achieve the elegant curved tapers shown in Mr Lees' drawing means there is no flat surface for the fixing nuts. My solution was to mill semicircular recesses for the nuts, which came out looking very nice. Note that if you do this you must use 'one size smaller' 6BA nuts – full size ones will fit, but people may wonder where the full size makers got a large enough pair of needle-nose pliers to tighten them up! The smaller nuts have sufficient space around them to allow one to imagine a spanner doing the task. The bearing brasses are just simple bobbin shapes (fig. 20). The drawing shows them with a flange on only one side (at least one of them is shown this way), I think this is a drafting error. They are drilled rather than reamed as the shaft is a non-standard size and they are too small to bore to size.

The old drawing appears to show a raised feature on top of each bearing cap. Presumably this is to do with lubrication, and could be as simple as a raised surface with an oil hole in it. This seems an invitation for dirt to enter the bearing, so small turned oil pots were made and fitted (photo 19). I made one with a removable cap and real cotton trimmings inside – but dummy ones (fig. 21) look better! I have since seen some later examples of cast-in lubricators with a hexagon-headed cap. This could be a more appropriate alternative, then again if such an engine were scrapped it would be the brass accessories like lubricators that would be salvaged or snaffled!

Next I'll take a look at the connecting rod, which means working on some very tiny bits of metal indeed.

Chapter 5: Connecting Rod

Norden's connecting rod is described as being fish bellied (the drawing allows it to be either flat or round) with strap and cotter bearings at each end Mr Lees' drawing is not exactly rich in details (the connecting rod is drawn as a piece with the crosshead!). I spent a long time searching out pictures of old stationary engines in the hope of getting a clear idea of what this meant in practice and what would be good proportions. In the end Anthony Mount's drawings for *Fairbairn's Column Engine* and Colin Pape's photographs of *Oliver Evan's Half Beam Engine* helped. Their connecting rods were of similar form, and gave me the guidance I needed on fair proportions. I have assumed a round shape and with a belly such that it approaches but does not contact the ends of the guide bars. The size scales to about 2" diameter in the centre. The connecting rod has strap and cotter connections at both ends, at 2' 1" centres (fig. 22).

As the rod needs to be forked to fit around the crosshead, this means that three strap and cotter bearings are needed. Due to the small size I decided not to split the bearings, but even so this meant three bearings, three straps and nine cotter parts.

With a little trepidation I decided to turn the rod from the solid, but discovered that this was actually a quite straightforward process. A blank was cut from 1/4" free machining steel plate, a centre drilled in one end and the other held in the 4-jaw chuck.

The fish belly was formed using a v-pointed tool (photo 20). Using this to turn the conical sections left a conical bevel at each end. I also left a short central cylindrical portion. I then, very carefully, used a series of fine and finer files to blend the tapers at the ends of the rod into the, finally finishing with wet and dry paper (photo 21). Files must always be used with a well fitting handle, even needle files; if you choose to use files to shape rotating work this is even more important. Although I have fitted handles on most of my needle files, I have a handle with an integral collet that can rapidly be exchanged between the others. A warning may be appropriate here – do not rely on the 'dipped plastic' type of handle as found on small diamond files, for example. The end of the file handle can burst out of the dipping, as I found out through a close call.

Before removing the embryo rod from the lathe, the outside of each end was turned to size. By comparing the widths of the flat surfaces remaining on each side of the work, it was clear the rod was slightly off-centre. This was not important as the final thickness of the bearing ends needed to be rather less than 1/4". After measurement, a skim of just over 20 thou was taken off the 'full' side of the embryo rod in the milling machine, to balance things up. The sides of the big end bearing were squared off (as they would have to fit between flanges on the bearing bush), but those on the fork were simply blended into the taper with a file.

Grooves for the bearing bushes were milled into each end of the connecting rod using a bull-nosed cutter (fig. 23). This required accurate setting of the rod in a machine vice, and the use of an edge finder to ensure the cutter was truly central. Care was taken to ensure the centre to centre distance would be as close to the nominal 2.08" (a scale 2' 1") as possible.

The centre of the fork was opened up by drilling, sawing and filing, rather than milling. The final step to complete the rod was making holes for the cotters. I decided on milling with a 1/16" end mill, followed by filing to final shape and size. Due to the depth of the slots (almost the same as the length of the end mill!) this was a slow process taken with great care (15-20 thou cuts). I scribed a line for one end of each slot, then held the rod in a machine vice. The cutter was gently advanced to the scribed line and the index set to zero. I then took a light cut to establish the length of the cut, and noted the index reading.

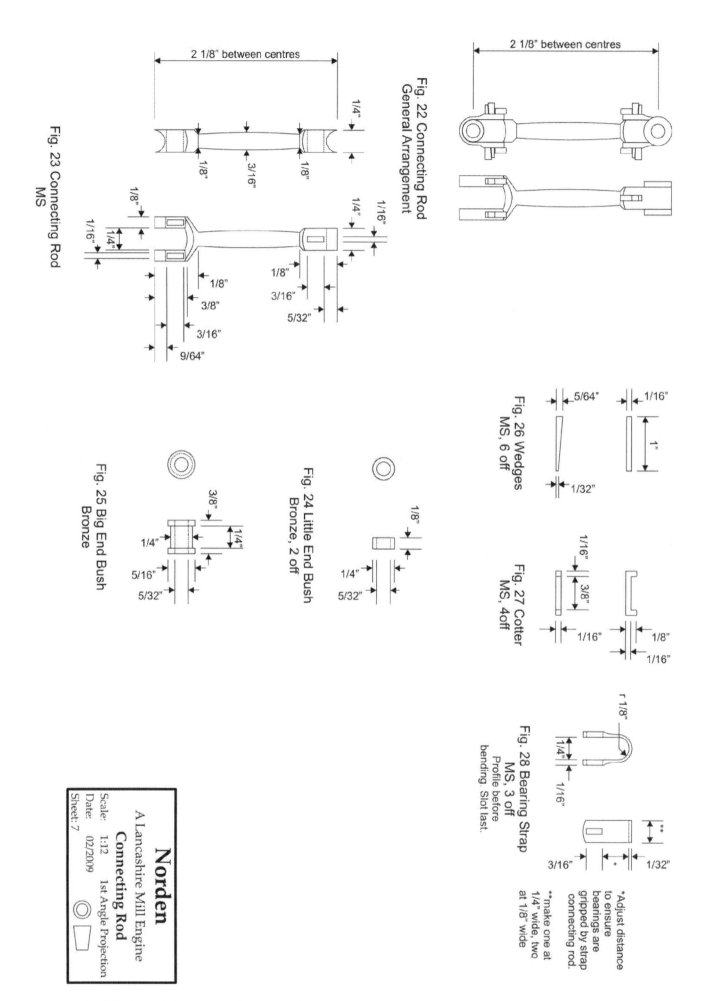

Fig. 22 Connecting Rod
General Arrangement

2 1/8" between centres

2 1/8" between centres

1/4"
1/8"
3/16"
1/8"

Fig. 23 Connecting Rod
MS

1/8"
1/4"
1/16"
1/8"
3/8"
3/16"
9/64"

1/4"
1/16"
1/8"
3/16"
5/32"

Fig. 25 Big End Bush
Bronze

3/8"
1/4"
5/16"
5/32"

Fig. 24 Little End Bush
Bronze, 2 off

1/8"
1/4"
5/32"

Fig. 26 Wedges
MS, 6 off

5/64"
1/16"
1"
1/32"

Fig. 27 Cotter
MS, 4off

1/16"
3/8"
1/16"
1/8"
1/16"

Fig. 28 Bearing Strap
MS, 3 off
Profile before
bending. Slot last.

r 1/8"
1/4"
1/16"
3/16"
*
1/32"

*Adjust distance
to ensure
bearings are
gripped by strap
connecting rod.

**make one at
1/4" wide, two
at 1/8" wide

Norden
A Lancashire Mill Engine
Connecting Rod

Scale: 1:12
Date: 02/2009   1st Angle Projection
Sheet: 7

Due to backlash and the cutter diameter, these readings were significantly closer together than the length of the slots. Further cuts were made by moving the cutter back and forth between zero and the second reading.

For subsequent slots in both the rod and the straps the procedure followed was exactly the same, using zero and the same second reading. This ensured that the initial slots were all exactly the same size. Squaring the slots off is a fiddly job, as only the tip would enter the slot. Making the three slots in the connecting rod took a whole evening. I have since discovered and used Colin Pape's cunning wheeze of drilling an axial hole down the centre of the rod, to reduce the amount of material to be removed.

Because of the small size, I did not make split bearings for the big and little ends (photos 22,23). The small ends are short tubes (fig. 24), whilst the big end bearing is a 'bobbin' shape (fig. 25). The bearings were scored to create the impression of a split instead. The bores of the bearing brasses were finish-reamed to size after parting them from the stock.

The straps are a task needing some care. The basic, flat, strap was easily cut and filled to size from 1/16" sheet, then 'waisted' slightly in the centre (fig. 28). An initial attempt to bend one to shape using a bar and a grooved die in the vice failed – the steel split along its length! Hammering the strap over a bar, then squeezing the ends in the vice was more effective, but due to work hardening I had to anneal each strap before it was possible to get the final shape, using pliers to bend it to shape around a bar in the vice. The end result was a surprisingly good fit for each strap, but after heat treatment they looked terrible. Some draw filing and polishing with abrasive paper was needed to make them look presentable. With the brasses in place it was straightforward to mark off the position of the slots in the straps (allowing a small space to ensure the straps would be under tension with the cotters fitted). Milling out the slots was, again, a slow and careful process, though with thinner material only a mere five cuts were needed to make each slot. Once finished, the straps were trimmed to length and give a final tidy up and polish.

There seem to be two full-size approaches to cotters. One of these is a notched bar that stops the strap from spreading and two wedges (*Fairbairn's Column Engine*), or a notched bar with one edge sloping and one wedge (*Oliver Evan's Half Beam* and Tubal Cain's beam engine *Lady Stephanie*). Despite the small size I decided to use the three-part solution (figs. 26,27).

The cotters are long, thin wedges filed up from strips of 1/16" steel. This is as near to 'wrist watch works' as I care to get. My small vice, which has quite sharp edges to its jaws was used to hold the parts. The wedges were shaped by holding a narrow strip of 1/16" steel at an angle to the top of the jaws, then filing until the tip was sharp. Each part was finished by draw filing with a 400 grit diamond file and rubbing over with fine wet and dry paper. A fair bit of fettling was required to make the slots big enough and the 'notched bars' small enough so that everything would go together. It was both surprising and satisfying to discover that once assembled even fairly gently, the bearing brasses were held quite firmly, testifying to the mechanical advantage provided by a wedge.

Once everything had been well fitted and allowed to run in and settle down, the straps and wedges were cut to length, filed fair and brought to a polish. It is a salutary thought that my little Trojan engine has its connecting rod in a single piece of gunmetal. The one I made for this engine has a total of sixteen pieces, but like the prototype, if there is ever any wear, replacing a bearing brass is a straightforward task.

Next we will look at two very distinctive features of the engine – the crosshead and its guides.

The crosshead is of the alligator-type and runs between locomotive-type slide bars, which are 2 ft. 3 1/2 in. long by 2 1/4 in. wide.

This is the locomotive style of crosshead that has a central pin between two bearing surfaces that run between parallel guide bars, attached to the cylinder top cover. The slide bars are drawn only supported at the base. As the crosshead has to fit the bars, it makes sense to start with them (fig. 29). The drawing gives a good indication of the appearance of the guide bars, which are t-shaped in cross section, and appear to be attached to the cylinder cover by base plates. These base plates are shown as very thick in one view, yet are absent in the other. I assumed that they would be substantial, but perhaps not of the enormous thickness implied by the front elevation. The most obvious shape would be to match the oval shape of the top-cover - why else have the little support brackets moulded in to the cylinder, if not to brace the slide bars? The shape almost decides itself, because of the position of the top-cover fixing studs, as each slide bar is held by two of these. The other dimensions were easy to arrive at starting from the width, which scales to exactly to 3/16".

The one definite change from the drawing was leaving out the 'waist' at the base of each slide bar. I find it hard to believe that any real-world engineer would build in a weakness at this most stressed point of the part. I also had to consider if a third fixing stud would be used at the 'tip' of each flange. Space was tight. On reflection, I realised that only forces spreading them outwards would ever stress the slide bars. An extra fixing here would do nothing, as long as the quality of fit was sufficient to ensure no movement in the joint between slide bar and top cover.

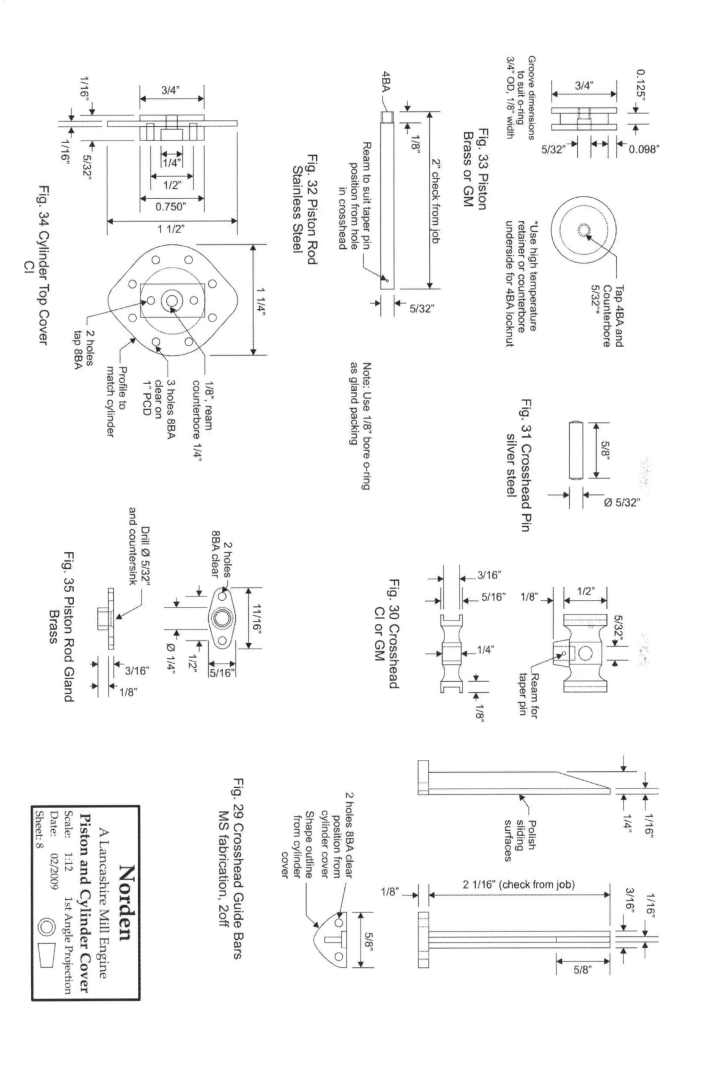

I cut four strips of 1/16" steel flat to just over 3/16" wide by 2 1/2" long, then milled a 1/16" wide groove down the centreline of two of them. The bases were cut and filed to shape from 1/8" steel, and short notches 1/16" wide milled at right angles to the flat side. I filed a small tab on one end of each ungrooved strip, and found that with a little gentle persuasion the two guide bars would slot together and remain in place. Risking all, I silver soldered each assembly in turn without any clamping. This was successful, and the raw machined finish of the slots with the filed edges of the strips allowed easy penetration of the solder (photo 27).

The heat of soldering had slightly distorted the bars so, using engineer's blue to highlight high spots, they were flattened by rubbing on the face of a smooth file and finished on wet and dry paper over a flat plate. Finally the three arms of the 'T' were milled to size and the base milled so that it was a true right angle to the slide faces (photo 28). Final fitting to the end covers was done by hand, noting that the ends of the stuffing box fixed their spacing. I had already discovered, by means of CAD, that, if made as long as the 2.292" scale dimension, the connecting rod might foul the ends of the bars, so they were left untrimmed to await a trial run with the various rods in place.

Cast iron would be the most likely material for the prototype's crosshead (fig. 30). As the slide bars were steel, and I felt that brass or gunmetal would be inappropriate, I decided to go ahead and use cast iron. Lightly stressed, this should have a lifetime as long as the entire engine. At this point I should come clean and admit that, in producing the final cross head I succeeded in making 11 scrappers and rejects (is this a record?) I learnt quite a bit about machining small flanges in brittle cast-iron as well as the care needed to achieve symmetrical results. The spacing of the slide bars was fixed at 0.250" by the size of the stuffing box on the top cover, so the starting point was a block of cast iron 5/8" wide. I got through many of these, each thick and long enough to contain the whole crosshead. I rapidly found it essential to ensure the block was completely square on each face, and also the need to start with fine-grained iron to cut them from.

The first machining operation was to mill slots on opposite sides of the block to fit the guide bars. Instead of trying to get an exact alignment relative to the sides of the block, I found it easier to mill one slot a near central to the block as possible. I then rotated the block without moving the mill Y-axis and milled out the second slot. I found I was able to remove and re-insert the block in the milling vice to measure progress and make the spacing of the two slots exactly right. The truth of the slots was checked by doing a dry-run assembly of the slide bars.

This temporary set up also allowed me to spot through the top cover to locate a hole for the piston rod. I then opened out a hole to a tight push fit on the piston rod. In due course a taper pin would be fitted to make this joint properly secure. A wedge might be closer to full scale practice, but I was worried about compromising the strength of the socket.

I then milled the inner and outer sides of the crosshead to leave a thin flange on either side of each slot, and to reduce the thickness of the central portion. A further cut was taken to thin the area where the wrist pin would be fitted, and some further cosmetic cuts taken with a round-nosed mill. As a final machining operation, a push-fit hole for the ground stainless steel wrist pin (fig.31) was made and the ends of the part milled to length.

Finishing of the crosshead was done by hand with needle files. I started by removing and shaping the areas either side of the piston rod socket, and ended by rounding off corners to give the appearance of a casting.

Perhaps, as a warning to others, I ought to document why I had so many failures. Aside from a few early attempts that were simply ill-proportioned, the main problems were poor alignment and the chipping off of the delicate edges of the grooves. The answer to both problems was simply patience and care. An alternative and easier construction method would have been to use steel and fit bronze slippers in the bottom of the grooves, or just to make the crosshead from brass or gunmetal.

The piston itself and the piston rod were considerably simpler to make. The piston (fig. 33) is turned from brass rod to an easy fit in the cylinder (the o-ring is what makes the seal). I fitted it to the piston rod (fig.32) before turning the outer diameter of the piston in position - note the short counterbore. The hole for the securing taper pin should be drilled with the piston rod fitted to the crosshead – after adjusting it to length.

On a trial erection of the engine (photo 27), I found that I had to do quite a lot of fettling to get the crosshead to run smoothly in the guide bars. I then had to go through most of this all over again once everything was painted! In the end a small amount of play is needed –the cross head needs to be a running fit and the guides must be truly parallel and not squeeze the crosshead at all (photo 28).

Next we move on to the cylinder, another very distinctive part of this engine.

Chapter 7: Cylinder

The cylinder is bolted direct to the bedplate by its bottom flange. The bore is approximately 9 in. and the stroke is 13 in.

The unusually shaped cylinder is one of the attractive features of the engine (fig. 36). Mr Lees' sizes of bore and stroke fit the external dimensions of the cylinder as drawn, and the stroke is consistent with the illustrated dimensions of the connecting rod and crank. The drawing shows that the cylinder top and upper cover have 'ears' to support the slide bars, but the base of the bars is not extended to allow an extra bolt or stud on the 'ears'. There is also a raised band around the cylinder. Possibly ornamental, this may also conceal a cast-in passageway to allow the exhaust to partially 'jacket' the cylinder. The cylinder is clearly shown as bolted directly to the bedplate by its bottom flange. This is a feature common with other engines of the period but creates issues regarding the bolts below the valve face. I suspect the steam chest may not have carried on down as close to the base of the cylinder in reality, but I decided to follow the drawing.

The cylinder pattern is a composite of several materials. The main part is an aluminium cylinder, with 1/2" diameter spigots at each end as core prints. The end flanges were cut and filed from perspex. One is circular, the other is rugby-ball shaped, to provide attachment points for the slide bars. The valve face has a pine core, though the sliding face was tidied up with a sheet of 2mm plywood. To make a smooth transition from the cylinder to the sides of the valve face, a sheet of thin aluminium sheet was wrapped around the entire assembly. Two perspex brackets were added under the 'ears' of the upper flange.

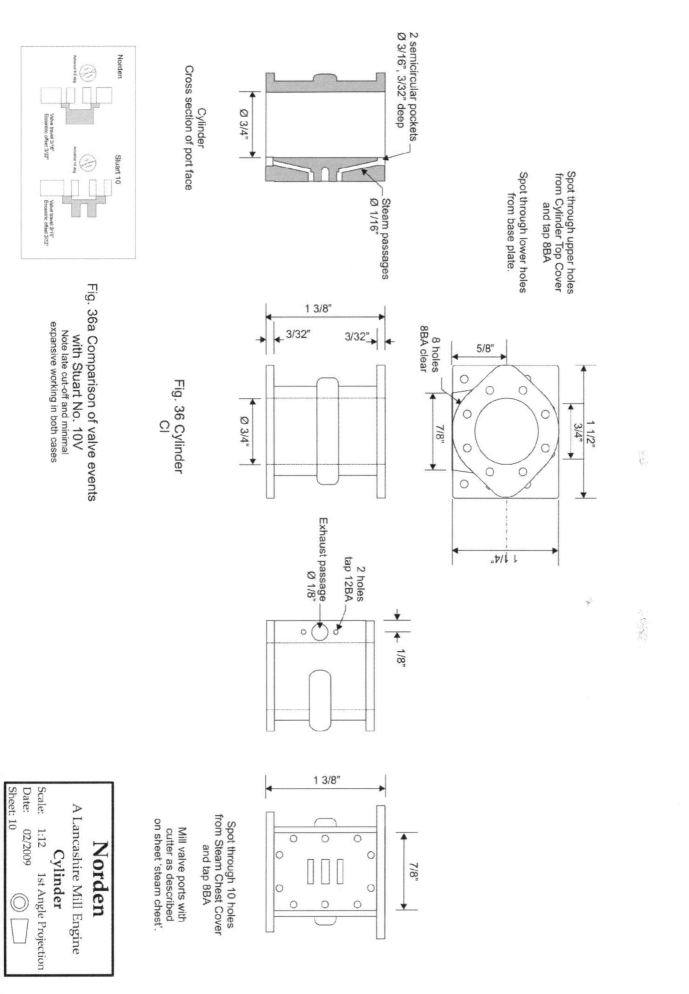

2 semicircular pockets
Ø 3/16", 3/32" deep

Cylinder
Cross section of port face

Ø 3/4"

Steam passages
Ø 1/16"

Spot through upper holes
from Cylinder Top Cover
and tap 8BA

Spot through lower holes
from base plate.

Fig. 36a Comparison of valve events
with Stuart No. 10V
Note late cut-off and minimal
expansive working in both cases

Norden

Exhaust 9 deg

Valve travel 3/16"
Eccentric offset 3/32"

Stuart 10

Admission 10 deg

Valve travel 3/16"
Eccentric offset 3/32"

Fig. 36 Cylinder
CI

1 3/8"

3/32"   3/32"

Ø 3/4"

8 holes
8BA clear

5/8"

7/8"

3/4"

1 1/2"

1 1/4"

Exhaust passage
Ø 1/8"

2 holes
tap 12BA

1/8"

1 3/8"

7/8"

Spot through 10 holes
from Steam Chest Cover
and tap 8BA

Mill valve ports with
cutter as described
on sheet 'steam chest'.

Norden
A Lancashire Mill Engine
Cylinder

Scale: 1:12   1st Angle Projection
Date: 02/2009
Sheet: 10

The final finishing touch is the raised band around the middle of the cylinder. This is the sole decorative element on what is otherwise a very functional engine. A 1/4" aluminium rod was milled to a semi-circular profile and annealed. This was done by smearing it with soap, and heating until the soap went black. The annealed material easily wrapped around the rest of the pattern, it was cut to length and filed round at the ends.

I assembled everything with superglue and five-minute epoxy, aside from wood-wood joints which were aliphatic resin. Epoxy has the advantage that it can be used to form a small fillet inside sharp corners. The pattern was finished with black acrylic paint.

The casting was reasonably successful, although the foundry chose a different line to split it to the one I had anticipated (photo 29). I have since improved the pattern to remove some acute corners, again the pattern is with Blackgates Engineering who can supply castings. After basic cleaning up of the casting by filing, it was held in a four-jaw chuck and faced parallel at each end (photo 30). With the square base firmly held in the chuck, it was bored out to 3/4" (scale for 9"). I took all cuts under self-act with a stout boring tool and a round-edged tool, and finished with two or three fine cuts at the final setting. The cast iron took a lovely satin finish on the bore.

The valve face could have been finished in the lathe, but I chose to finish it by flycutting in the milling machine. This is slower but gives a good finish that needs only gentle polishing on wet and dry paper over a surface plate to create a perfect valve face.

I had to decide on my own valve dimensions; the valve travel is the same as both the *Stuart No. 10* and *Trojan* at 3/16". I meddled with the timings to reduce the exhaust lap and make the cutoff later, in order to favour running on low pressure air. This seems to have worked. I decided on steam port width and spacing of 1/16", exhaust port width of 3/32" and port length: 5/16" (fig. 40). The ports can be milled out, but for guaranteed accuracy there is nothing to beat a ganged cutter as advocated by LBSC (and others).

A small diameter cutter is needed, in order to get a reasonable port depth (the smaller the cutter diameter the deeper the ports it cuts). In this case to get a width of 5/16 and a depth of approximately 1/16" a cutter from 3/8" silver steel was chosen. Using a 1/16" wide parting tool I made a tool blank in the form of three disks on a shank. The end disks being 1/16" wide and the centre disk 3/32" wide. The shank had to be long enough to clear the entire slide face and the top flange (fig. 41).

I milled six teeth on the cutter following a sketch by Edgar Westbury in his M.E. series on 'Unicorn'. This requires milling large 'bites' with the cutter lined up on the centre line of the blank, in order to create pointed teeth with no top rake, and a very small witness at the tip (photo 31). With the cutter running fast, but with a slow feed I had no problems with 'grab'. I indexed the blank by eye, as uneven tooth spacing is actually an advantage in this type of cutter, reducing the danger of resonant effects causing chatter. I carefully cleaned up the sides of the teeth with a file. I hardened the whole cutter then tempered it in the oven. I wanted to temper it a bit further than the usual pale straw, as it looked very fragile. I decided to start at gas mark seven (which is supposed to be about 220°/pale straw) knowing the oven thermostat was inaccurate by about one mark. This was just as well, as after a false start (my wife turned off the 'empty' oven), the cutter came out an even pale bronze colour that probably equates to dark straw. I used a diamond slip to clean up the sides of the teeth and to put a shine on the cutting faces.

I clamped the cylinder in a milling vice (you could equally clamp it to the milling table or to the vertical slide on a lathe), with the valve face perpendicular to the long axis of the table. I used an edge finder to locate one side of the valve face. This is a 'ball on a stick' which when spinning over a surface stays still, until they are precisely aligned, when it 'runs' along the surface. My ball is meant to be .250", but I miked mine at .248". A difference well worth being aware of if you are going to the bother of using such an aid to setting up! I advanced the cross slide by half the width of the valve face plus half the width of the ball. I now had to fiddle a bit to get the cutter exactly half way up the valve face, ensuring the chuck would clear the fixing bolt.

I was very apprehensive that such a delicate looking cutter would bend or break if it dug into the work. With two sets of teeth in the work at once the total cut length would be 7/16" of cutting edge, an awful lot for a tool shank about 3/16" in diameter. I ran the cutter at about 500 rpm, and fed the work into it very, very slowly (fig. 42). To my satisfaction, the swarf came out more like fine dust than chips, building into a neat cone below the cylinder (photo 32). The result was absolutely perfect, far better than I could have achieved with an end mill (photo 33). It seems like the old guard knew a thing or two.

I used a milling vice to hold the cylinder (protected by aluminium slips) and used a 1/8" FC3 cutter to mill the 3/32" deep recesses at each end of the cylinder (photo 34). I then used a tilting vice to hold the casting at an angle to drill the steam passages number 53. I marked the position of the upper valve port on the side of the cylinder in pencil, and repeatedly moved the tip of the drill from in the recess to alongside the cylinder to ensure that it would break out into the port without damaging the face. It is essential that the drill neatly enters the corner of the recess for this to be successful (photo 35). If you feed too fast or the drill is out of line when it starts, it will wander and could either snap, miss the port or, worst of all, emerge in the port face. I used a depth stop on the mill, and the drill neatly entered one side of the port. Without altering the angle of the vice I inverted the cylinder and drilled the other steam passage.

This is a rather nerve-racking procedure. Try to err on the side of drilling at too shallow an angle, as if you miss the port you can 'poke' a 1/16" drill into the bottom of each port to link it to he passage. If you use an end mill to create your ports, you can make them a little deeper and the job becomes less critical - you can make a wooden 'cradle' to hold the cylinder for drilling as you won't need to make small adjustments to the angle.

The final task at this stage was to drill the exhaust port, a less critical operation, as all I had to do is drill parallel to the valve face and avoid breaking into the cylinder bore. The only danger is breaking the drill as it emerges into the port.

The bottom cover for the cylinder was the base plate. Spotting through for the cylinder studs was a small challenge. I made a tiny centre punch from a rod that was a good fit in the holes in the cylinder

The top cover casting was something of a disappointment –my pattern lacked the block on top for the gland. I milled and turned a new cover (fig. 34) from another piece of scrap cast iron. I filed it to fit the 'eared' shape of the cylinder top flange before milling the rectangular piston gland against which the guide bars fit. I have now made a new and better pattern, which includes a chucking piece to simplify machining.

With the cylinder in the four-jaw chuck, I used superglue to hold the top cover in place and spotted through tapping size for the cylinder bolts with a rotary table.

The piston was turned from a 1" brass blank, in place on its rod. In a deliberate departure from full scale practice, I put a single groove around the piston and fitted a silicon ring. It may be the coward's way out, but for an engine that will only run at low pressures on air or steam, this is a simple way to get a piston that seals well but runs freely.

The piston rod gland (fig. 35) is barely hinted at in the drawings. I used an elliptical gland typical of 18th century engines, but have substituted a silicone ring for packing material. The hole in the gland appears oversize, but this is because the top of the hole has been chamfered, allowing oil on the piston rod to collect and be re-applied to the rod as it reciprocates, rather than being scraped off. This was sometimes done in full size practice. A similar, but smaller arrangement was used for the valve rod gland.

The oval shape of the gland itself was achieved by first machining a thin disc with a central hollow spigot. The two holes for fixing studs were drilled and used to fix the embryo gland to a short section of 1" diameter steel, overlapping the edge. The gland was then machined down to the level of the steel, and reversed. This gives two neat long edges, and it is a simple job to file the ends neatly round using a filing button as a guide. The gland body itself (on top of the cylinder cover) should not be shaped to match the gland, as its rectangular shape locates the ends of the crosshead guides (photo 36).

With the cylinder complete, the next steps are the steam chest and the valve.

If we follow Mr Lees' drawing, then the steam chest is quite thin and the valve rod rather delicate. I decided that 1/4" thick was too thin to allow for a robust slide valve and an adequate gland, but 5/16" was sufficient, if machined to close tolerances (fig. 37).

My original pattern for the steam chest was too small – I have now made a larger pattern. I cut a short section out of a large chunk of iron, which had once been a guide for an industrial wood planing machine. This machined nicely, a 1/32" cut getting right under the 'skin'. I reduced the piece to 5/16" thick in the four-jaw chuck (photo 37), then to 7/8" wide. I skimmed the bottom of the chest to give a flat surface, and milled out the central cavity (photo 38). I removed as much metal as possible, except where the valve rod enters. The larger the steam-chest volume the better the engine will run as there will be a good charge of steam ready to fill the cylinder as soon as the valve opens, but take care to leave enough 'meat' for the fixing holes.

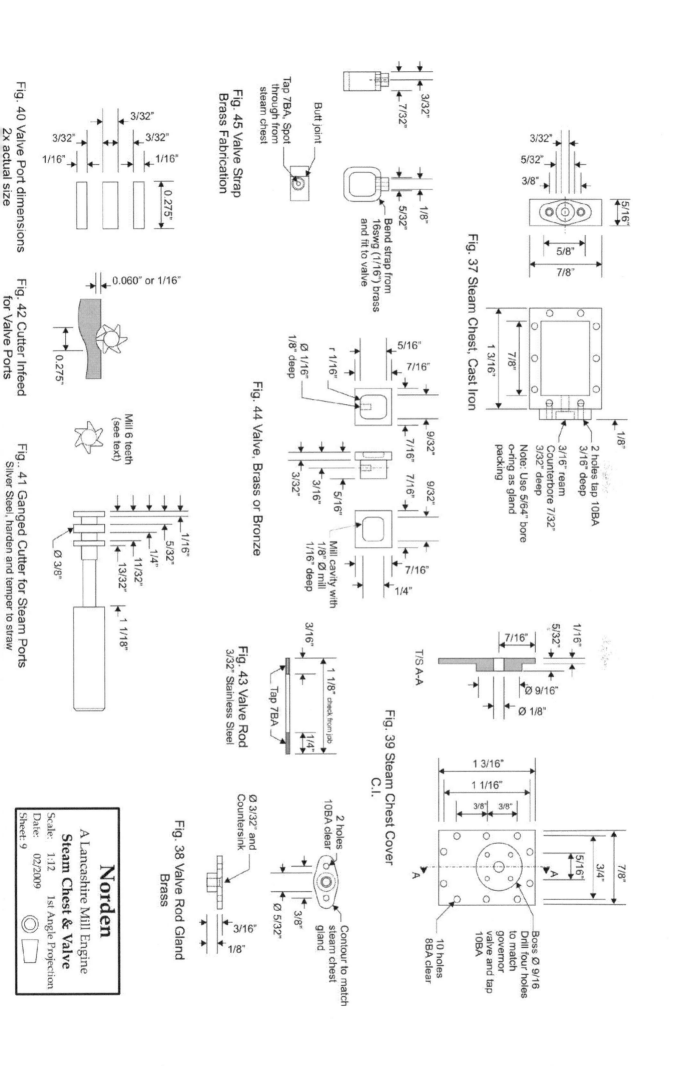

Fig. 40 Valve Port dimensions
2x actual size

3/32"   3/32"   3/32"
1/16"   1/16"
0.275"

Fig. 42 Cutter Infeed
for Valve Ports

0.060" or 1/16"
0.275"

Fig. 41 Ganged Cutter for Steam Ports
Silver Steel, harden and temper to straw

Mill 6 teeth
(see text)

Ø 3/8"

1/16"
5/32"
1/4"
11/32"
13/32"
1 1/18"

Fig. 45 Valve Strap
Brass Fabrication

3/32"
7/32"

Butt joint

Tap 7BA. Spot
through from
steam chest

1/8"
5/32"

Bend strap from
16swg (1/16") brass
and fit to valve

Fig. 44 Valve, Brass or Bronze

Ø 1/16"
1/8" deep

r 1/16"

5/16"
7/16"

9/32"
7/16"

7/16"
9/32"

3/16"
3/32"
5/16"

7/16"
1/4"

Mill cavity with
1/8" Ø mill
1/16" deep

Fig. 43 Valve Rod
3/32" Stainless Steel

3/16"

1 1/8" check from job
1/4"

Tap 7BA

Fig. 38 Valve Rod Gland
Brass

Ø 3/32" and
Countersink

3/16"
1/8"

Fig. 37 Steam Chest, Cast Iron

3/32"
5/32"
3/8"

5/16"

5/8"
7/8"

1 3/16"
7/8"

1/8"

2 holes tap 10BA
3/16" deep
Counterbore 7/32"
3/32" deep

3/16" ream

Note: Use 5/64" bore
o-ring as gland
packing

Fig. 39 Steam Chest Cover
C.I.

T/S A-A

7/16"
5/32"
1/16"

Ø 9/16"
Ø 1/8"

1 3/16"
1 1/16"
3/8"   3/8"

5/16"
3/4"
7/8"

A   A

2 holes
10BA clear

3/8"
5/32"

Contour to match
steam chest
gland

10 holes
8BA clear

Boss Ø 9/16
Drill four holes
to match
governor
valve and tap
10BA

Norden
A Lancashire Mill Engine
Steam Chest & Valve

Scale: 1:12   1st Angle Projection
Date: 02/2009
Sheet: 9

Mr Lees' drawing does not give a very convincing representation of the valve gland (fig. 38). On an engine of this age an oval gland fixed by a pair of studs would be likely. The oval gland was machined in the same way as that described for the piston rod gland (photo 39). This was then used as a template for hand-shaping the gland body on the steam chest by filing (photo 40). The new pattern should result in castings with a well-formed gland body.

The cover is simpler than it appears (fig. 39). First I machined it so it the thickness of the cover over the boss, then using the four-jaw chuck it was reduced to a rectangle the same size as the steam chest. A hole was drilled where the centre of the boss is located, and this was used to mount it on a screwed mandrel for turning the boss. I drilled the mounting holes using co-ordinates on my milling machine, but only at tapping size.

The next step was to assemble the cover, steam chest and cylinder using double-sided tape and a clamp. Using the cover as a guide the tapping holes for the studs where drilled through the chest into the valve face of the cylinder (photo 41). The holes in the cover and steam chest were opened up to clearance size. The final task on the steam chest is to drill and tap the steam inlet. At this point I tapped the holes in the valve face (photo 42).

I originally drilled the valve gland 1/8" counterbored 1/4" for a silicone sealing ring on a 1/8" rod, but inspection of the drawings and other prototypes suggested that, though delicate, the full size rod was probably no more than 1" diameter, and possibly less. The closest imperial size would be 5/64" – not an easily obtained size. 3/32" seemed decidedly clumsy, so 1/16" was decided upon. This is also the size that Tubal Cain chose for the slide valve of *Lady Stephanie* – an engine to the same scale with a similarly proportioned valve. Turning this into an opportunity, a closely fitting brass bush drilled 1/16" and counterbored 3/16" was turned up and fitted to the hole.

I think we can fairly assume the valve rod was a plain rod, threaded for adjustment (Fig. 43). Thinned down slightly at the ends and threaded 8BA this gives reasonable adjustment for the slide valve. As mentioned earlier, the steam chest is not very deep. This means there is a distinct shortage of space for the typical 'four pronged valve' design. Fortunately Curly came to my rescue – in his design for the *Titfield Thunderbolt* he uses a rectangular strap that wraps around the valve body with a boss at one end. This design represents one type of full-size practice, noting that it only applies to engines where there is no tail guide for the valve rod. It is ideally suited to a low profile assembly using a light valve rod.

I mentioned the valve port design last time. The diagram (fig. 36a) is one I created to help me visualise the valve events, it shows how the smaller valve cavity and shorter valve of *Norden* compared with the *No.10* favours admission over exhaust. If I was intending an engine to work on steam, it would make sense to do the opposite as my valve design does not favour expansive working.

The valve itself was simple to construct (fig. 44). Once milled to the outer dimensions, I used a 4mm ball-nosed end mill to open up the valve space to a depth of just over 2mm (photo 43). An ordinary square-ended mill could be used, but a curved steam space is more likely to be prototypical. I then turned the valve over, gripping it carefully by the lower edges, reduced the central portion, and milled it to finished thickness. I rounded the corners of the central body by hand with a file.

The valve strap was made from a strip of hard brass, bent carefully to shape, with a joint a quarter of the way along the side bearing the boss (fig. 45). It was made to be a firm fit over the body of the valve, and then I drilled 1/16" through the strap and into the valve body. A 1/16" spigot was turned on the end of about 1" of 4mm (sorry!) brass to fit the hole. The two parts were silver soldered together simultaneously joining the two ends of the strap (photo 44).

With the strap fitted to the valve, and the steam chest (without cover) fitted to the cylinder, I carefully wedged the valve in position. I used slivers of 1mm ply on each side of the valve, and a block of brass scrap between it and the end of the steam chest. This made it possible to spot through the valve rod gland onto the strap boss, which was subsequently tapped 10BA for the valve rod. Some judicious file work on the strap and valve body ensured a free but close fit, to allow the valve to 'float' and seat properly on the valve face. The hole in the valve body was opened up to number 38, to ensure that the valve rod's tip could, if required, pass into the boss without restricting this floating action (photo 45).

Of course, the valve will do nothing without an eccentric and rod to drive it. These will be described next.

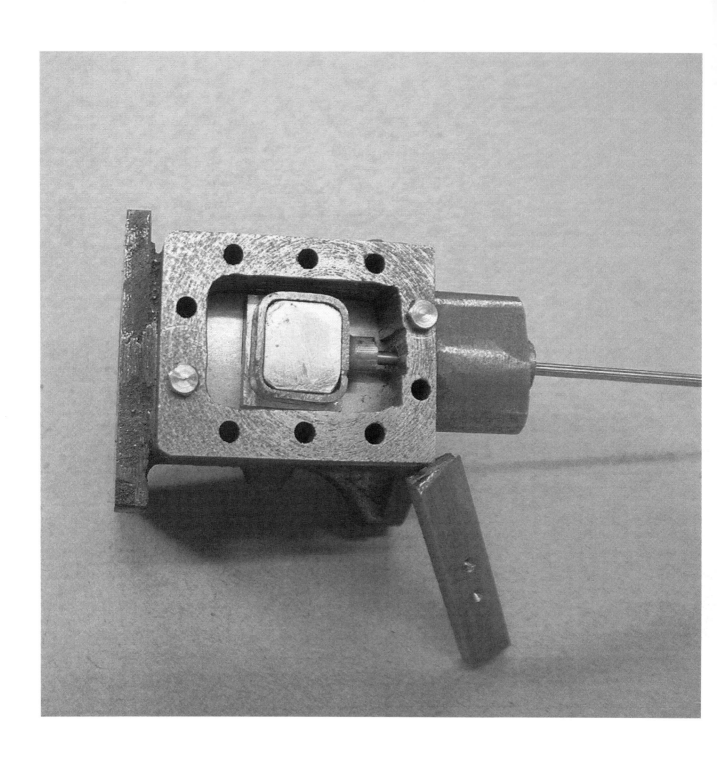

From Mr Lee's drawing we can assume a fixed eccentric valve drive. This arrangement is usual for an engine run at constant speed, and indeed the engine speed is controlled by a Watt governor, in an unusual (but rather sensible, it seems to me) position underneath the table.

The size of the eccentric strap is shown, but other dimensions are not clear from Mr Lees' sketch. The eccentric (fig. 46) was turned in the 4-jaw chuck from continuous cast iron to 0.750" and a groove 40 thou deep by the width of my narrowest parting tool put in all round. This is about the core diameter of a 10BA screw, allowing the use of such a screw as a locating peg. I set the cross-slide index to zero at the point where the tool just contacted the work, before making the cut.

There are various ways of obtaining the correct offset for the eccentric (in this case 3/32"). I suggest you use whatever method you are most comfortable with. I used a very simple method for the first time and it worked perfectly. First I withdrew the parting tool and then advanced it until it was at zero again. I then withdrew it by 3/32" (actually a little further than this, then back in again to allow for backlash). Now it was just a case of gently adjusting the chuck so that the tool just contacts the edge of the eccentric at its high point.

I then centred and drilled in a number of stages for the crankshaft, then using a round-nosed tool to create the boss on the side of the eccentric. The final task was parting off which, despite the interrupted cut, went without incident. I should admit to three 'scrappers' - one I decided was too small (photo 46), one I made without a boss which did not look right, and for the third I counted the index in the wrong direction and made the throw too great. Still, all three may serve for other engines in the future!

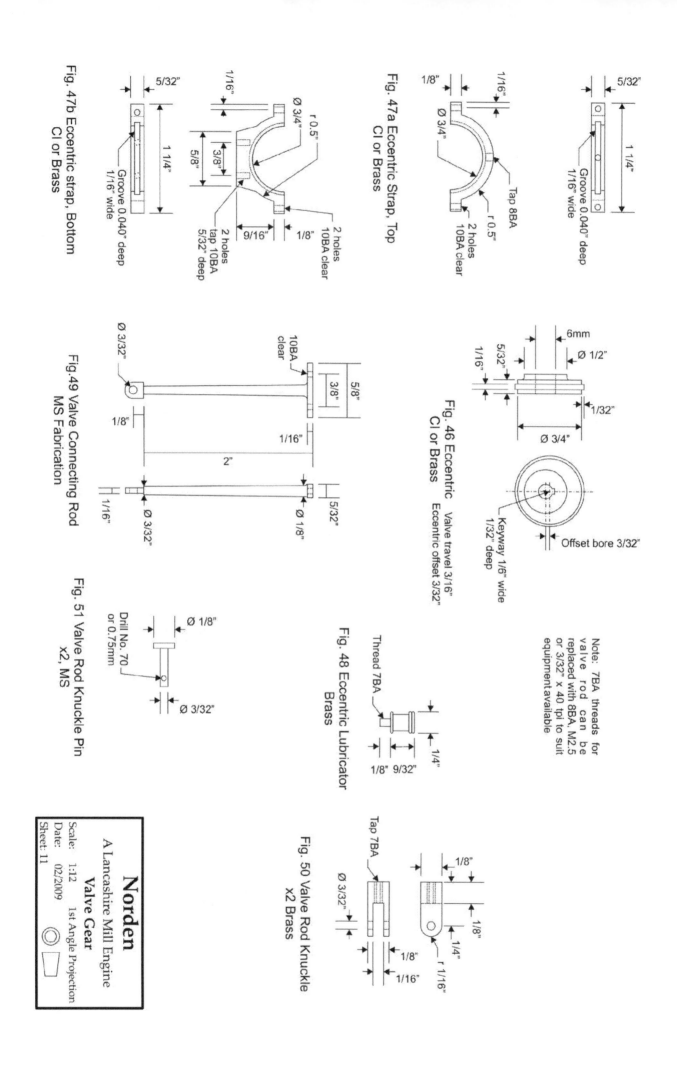

Fig. 47b Eccentric strap, Bottom
CI or Brass

Fig. 47a Eccentric Strap, Top
CI or Brass

5/32"

1/16"

Ø 3/4"

r 0.5"

5/8"

3/8"

Groove 0.040" deep
1/16" wide

1 1/4"

2 holes
tap 10BA
5/32" deep

9/16"   1/8"

2 holes
10BA clear

1/8"

1/16"

Ø 3/4"

r 0.5"

Tap 8BA

2 holes
10BA clear

5/32"

Groove 0.040" deep
1/16" wide

1 1/4"

Fig.49 Valve Connecting Rod
MS Fabrication

Ø 3/32"

10BA
clear

5/8"

3/8"

1/8"

1/16"

2"

1/16"

Ø 3/32"

Ø 1/8"

5/32"

Fig. 46 Eccentric   Valve travel 3/16"
CI or Brass   Eccentric offset 3/32"

6mm

5/32"

1/16"

Ø 1/2"

1/32"

Ø 3/4"

Keyway 1/16" wide
1/32" deep

Offset bore 3/32"

Note: 7BA threads for
valve rod can be
replaced with 8BA, M2.5
or 3/32" x 40 tpi to suit
equipment available

Fig. 51 Valve Rod Knuckle Pin
x2, MS

Drill No. 70
or 0.75mm

Ø 1/8"

Ø 3/32"

Fig. 48 Eccentric Lubricator
Brass

Thread 7BA

1/4"

1/8" 9/32"

Fig. 50 Valve Rod Knuckle
x2 Brass

Tap 7BA

Ø 3/32"

1/8"

1/8"

1/4"

1/8"

1/16"

r 1/16"

Norden
A Lancashire Mill Engine
Valve Gear

Scale: 1:12
Date: 02/2009
Sheet: 11

1st Angle Projection

I have drawn the eccentric with a raised flange around it which runs in a groove in the eccentric strap. An alternative, which may create a little less friction, is to machine a narrow groove around the eccentric and fit a suitable guide pin in the eccentric strap.

The eccentric strap (figs 47a, b) was also a prolific generator of scrap, though as with so many aspects of this project the failures were more like prototypes than disasters. I started with a number of brass straps, but these all looked toy-like. It had to be cast-iron for the strap. After a first attempt with the rim too narrow and fragile, I settled on what seems to be a typical design.

A piece of cast iron (though feel free to use a slice of brass bar) was sawn out of a lump of scrap and faced down to just above nominal size. It was then marked out and sawn into a cross-shape, the two narrow arms either side serving to take temporary fixings were drilled No. 43 - tight 8BA clearance. The blank was then drilled 1/2" before being cut in half, the joint surfaces cleaned up, and rejoined. The centre hole was then bored out to 0.751" using a boring head in the mill. A vice was used to hold the blank, so that the little 8BA screws were only serving for location. Before leaving the mill, a skim was taken from each surface to leave the blank parallel sided and matched in width to the eccentric.

If you are using a raised ridge on the eccentric, as drawn, then I suggest that you hold the strap in a four-jaw chuck and bore it in the lathe, following up by using a small, specially ground tool to create the internal 40 thou deep groove. Such a tool is easily made by turning a piece of 3/8" silver steel to 3//16" leaving a 1/16" thick disc on the end. File away half of the disc and then harden and temper the tool. It can now be held and used in the manner of a boring bar to cut the internal groove.

In the lathe an offcut of 1" brass bar was turned down to 7/8" and drilled 5mm. I then opened up the hole to 6mm for a few millimetres before parting off a thick slice. The end of the bar was then reduced to a firm push-fit in the embryo eccentric and tapped M6. Without taking the bar out of the chuck, it was transferred to a dividing head in the mill and the eccentric attached and clamped firmly in place with the aforementioned thick slice. It was now just a matter of careful handle-juggling to shape the outside of the eccentric, leaving a flat for the eccentric rod. Once shaped the eccentric was removed and drilled and tapped 10BA for the rod and the locating pin and 7BA (drilled right through No.60) for the oiler. With the two final fixing bolts fitted the ends were sawn off and everything tidied up nicely with a file (photo 47).

The little oiler adds a nice touch. I started with some 1/4" brass rod and turned a spigot to 0.091" OD. I slightly tapered the base of the body with a skewed tool then carefully drilling the spigot No.60. I then used a tailstock die holder to put on the 7BA screw, using the back of the tap to get thread as near to the body as possible. Using a narrow (3/64") parting tool I shaped the body of the oiler to suit.

I then made a small chucking piece from brass hexagon with a central hole tapped 7BA – I later marked the position of No.1 jaw so that I could re-use this jig. Working very carefully with the work screwed into this hole I faced off the end and drilled it out No. 29 and tapped it 3BA for a lid. I then removed it from the jig, shortened the threaded spigot and fitted it to the eccentric strap.

The lid is just a slice of brass bar with a 3BA thread and drilled No.60 for an air hole. I found that the number 60 hole was quite large enough for oil to run straight through. So following full-size practice I added a wick. Aided by a loop of thin iron wire I threaded four strands of nylon rigging cord through the oiler, trimming them carefully to length with a razor blade. A nice touch in case a judge ever unscrews the top of the oiler! Don't tell anyone though – the other oilers are dummies (fig. 48)!

The eccentric rod is drawn as quite delicate - about 1" diameter. In the absence of detail I have assumed a taper. My rod tapers from a scale 1 1/2" to 1 1/8" top to bottom (fig. 49). It may seem wasteful of stock, but I found the approach of brazing a rod into a much larger bar worked very well (photo 48). With the large end held in the three-jaw chuck I centred the small end, and then carefully turned the taper (photo 49).

All the drawing shows for the wrist joint is a simple block. I used a simple forked joint (fig. 50) screwed to the valve rod using a wrist pin (fig. 51) and secured in turn by a split pin. The eye for the joint was silver soldered to the end of the eccentric rod (photo 50). The hardest part of this was drilling the wrist pin – I used a hand held mini-drill and snapped a carbide drill before successfully doing the job with an ordinary HSS drill.

With the eccentric the basic working parts of the engine are complete (photo 51).

To finish it, the motor needs the governor, pipework and a few finishing touches.

The governor has two 5 in. diameter balls and was driven direct off the crankshaft by bevel gears to the tops of the governor spindle.

The governor is driven directly from the crankshaft by two large gears. These bevel gears are clearly drawn by Mr Lees as being of equal size, at 9" diameter, which is reasonable for running on a 2 1/2" shaft. The 1:1 governor gearing suggests the engine would have run at a modest speed of perhaps a hundred or more rpm, rather than 'ticking over' like a beam engine. The drawing has marks indicating teeth, possibly about 20, which gives a well-proportioned bevel, although it may be that the teeth were smaller and more numerous than this. I made two 20-tooth bevel gears (fig. 52, photo 52) using the constant-depth method described by Ivan Law in *Gears and Gear Cutting* Chapter 11, Workshop Practice Series, No 17.

They are completely silent at the speed the engine runs. I have considered replacing them with cast iron gears – either metal could be prototypical but cast iron would be more likely. One gear was fitted to the crankshaft, the other to the governor spindle.

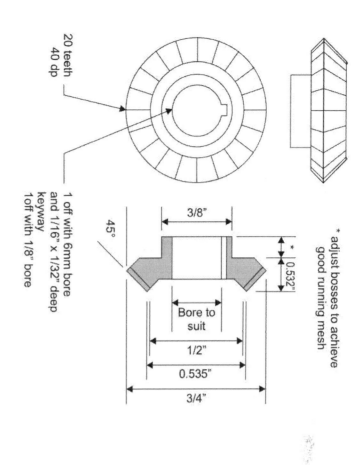

20 teeth
40 dp

1 off with 6mm bore
and 1/16" x 1/32" deep
keyway
1off with 1/8" bore

Fig. 52 Governor Bevel Gear
X2, Brass, MS or CI, 2 off

45°

3/8"

0.532" *

Bore to
suit

1/2"

0.535"

3/4"

* adjust bosses to achieve
good running mesh

Bevel Gear Specification

Information required to use Ivan Law's parallel depth
bevel method (*Gears and Gear Cutting*,Chapter 11,
Workshop Practice Series, No 17).

20 teeth, 40DP, 20° pressure angle
Blank Diameter: 0.75"
Cutter number: 4 (26-34 teeth)
Depth of cut: 0.054"
Blank roll: 1/80 revolution = 4.5°
Cutter offsets: +/- 0.020"

For home made cutter (*ibid*, chapter12) use the
dimensions below to make and use the form tool.

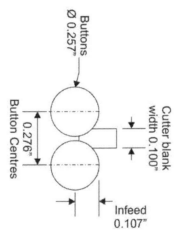

Buttons
Ø 0.257"

Cutter blank
width 0.100"

0.276"
Button Centres

Infeed
0.107"

Fig. 53 Form tool for gear cutters
X2

Note: Any pair of matching
45° bevel gears with an
overall diameter of about 3/4"
and bosses that can be
bored or bushed to a suitable
size may be used.

Norden
A Lancashire Mill Engine
Bevel Gears

Scale: 1:12
Date: 02/2009
Sheet: 12

1st Angle Projection

The information required to use Ivan Law's parallel depth bevel method is as follows:

20 teeth, 40DP, 20° pressure angle

Blank Diameter: 0.75"

Cutter number: 4 (26-34 teeth)

Depth of cut: 0.054"

Blank roll: 1/80 revolution = 4.5°

Cutter offsets: +/- 0.020"

For homemade cutter use the dimensions drawn (fig. 53) to make and use the form tool. If you don't wish to make your own gears, a pair of commercial bevel gears of 3/4" diameter can be bored out or bushed to suit. It is possible that Blackgates or other suppliers may have suitable pairs of gears available.

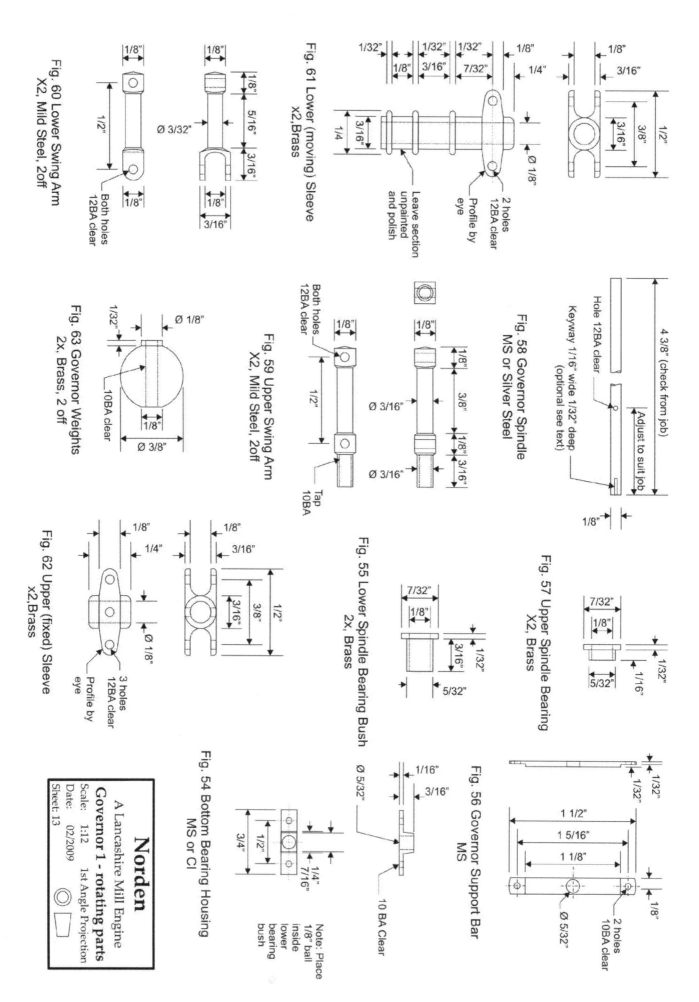

Fig. 60 Lower Swing Arm X2, Mild Steel, 2off

Both holes 12BA clear

1/8" · 1/2" · Ø 3/32" · 5/16" · 3/16" · 3/16" · 1/8"

Fig. 61 Lower (moving) Sleeve x2, Brass

2 holes 12BA clear
Profile by eye
Leave section unpainted and polish

1/32" · 1/8" · 1/32" · 1/32" · 3/16" · 7/32" · 1/8" · 1/4" · 1/8" · 3/16"

3/16" · 1/4" · Ø 1/8" · 3/8" · 3/16" · 1/2"

Fig. 63 Governor Weights 2x, Brass, 2 off

10BA clear
Ø 1/8" · 1/32" · 1/8" · Ø 3/8"

Fig. 59 Upper Swing Arm X2, Mild Steel, 2off

Both holes 12BA clear
Tap 10BA

1/8" · 1/2" · Ø 3/16" · 3/8" · 1/8" · 3/16" · Ø 3/16"

Fig. 58 Governor Spindle MS or Silver Steel

Hole 12BA clear
Keyway 1/16" wide 1/32" deep (optional see text)
4 3/8" (check from job)
Adjust to suit job
1/8"

Fig. 62 Upper (fixed) Sleeve x2, Brass

3 holes 12BA clear
Profile by eye

1/8" · 1/4" · 1/8" · 3/16" · Ø 1/8" · 3/16" · 3/8" · 1/2"

Fig. 55 Lower Spindle Bearing Bush 2x, Brass

7/32" · 1/8" · 1/32" · 3/16" · 5/32"

Fig. 57 Upper Spindle Bearing X2, Brass

7/32" · 1/8" · 1/32" · 1/16" · 5/32"

Fig. 54 Bottom Bearing Housing MS or CI

Ø 5/32" · 1/16" · 3/16"
Note: Place 1/8" ball inside lower bearing bush
10 BA Clear
3/4" · 1/2" · 1/4" · 7/16"

Fig. 56 Governor Support Bar MS

1/32" · 1/32" · 1 1/2" · 1 5/16" · 1 1/8" · 1/8" · Ø 5/32"
2 holes 10BA clear

Norden
A Lancashire Mill Engine
Governor 1 - rotating parts

Scale:	1:12
Date:	02/2009
Sheet:	13

1st Angle Projection

The vertical spindle runs in two brass bushes. As well as one mounted in the steel housing on the baseplate (figs 54, 55 & photo 53), there must have been a support just below the bevel gear to keep it in mesh. I have assumed a cross-piece (fig. 56) with a bearing bush (Fig. 57) attached on top of the table. None of these parts requires special explanation, though note that a 1/8" diameter steel ball should be dropped into the lower bush. Given the length of the spindle and the size of the governor balls a stout shaft (fig. 58) would be needed to ensure it did not flex, so 1/8" scaling to 3/4" on the prototype seems reasonable.

I made the four governor arms and links from 1/8" square steel rod (figs 59, 60). If you have the confidence and skill to use smaller sections, be my guest! Anthony Mount has given some very good advice in past issues on a slow and steady approach to such delicate parts. All the holes and the root of each fork were drilled before turning down the intermediate sections in the 4-jaw chuck. This ensures they are all aligned properly. The ends of the governor arms were drilled out and lengths of 10BA studding fitted on which to mount the governor balls. The final parts of the assembly are the fixed and sliding sleeves fitted on the spindle. The upper one of these is fixed and has two forks for the arms. The lower sleeve slides and has forks for the two lower links and a collar for the actuating fork (photo 54).

Making the sleeves (figs 61, 62) may appear tricky, but there is an easy way, if you take it steadily. Start with a section of 1/2" brass bar, centre it and drill 1/8" for the spindle. Mark out a 3/8" circle and scribe across with a sharp point at centre height. Now centre-pop where the diameter crosses the circle, and drill two more 1/8" holes to form the roots of the forks. Turn the spindle to shape, leaving a disk of metal for the forks. Use a parting tool to form the grooves between the raised rings. Mill or file off the sides of the disk, either side of the holes, then open up the embryo forks with a file. All that remains are the pivot holes. I got quite good at this as the first two lower sleeves I made were not long enough to ensure the follower groove was below the level of the balls at all times.

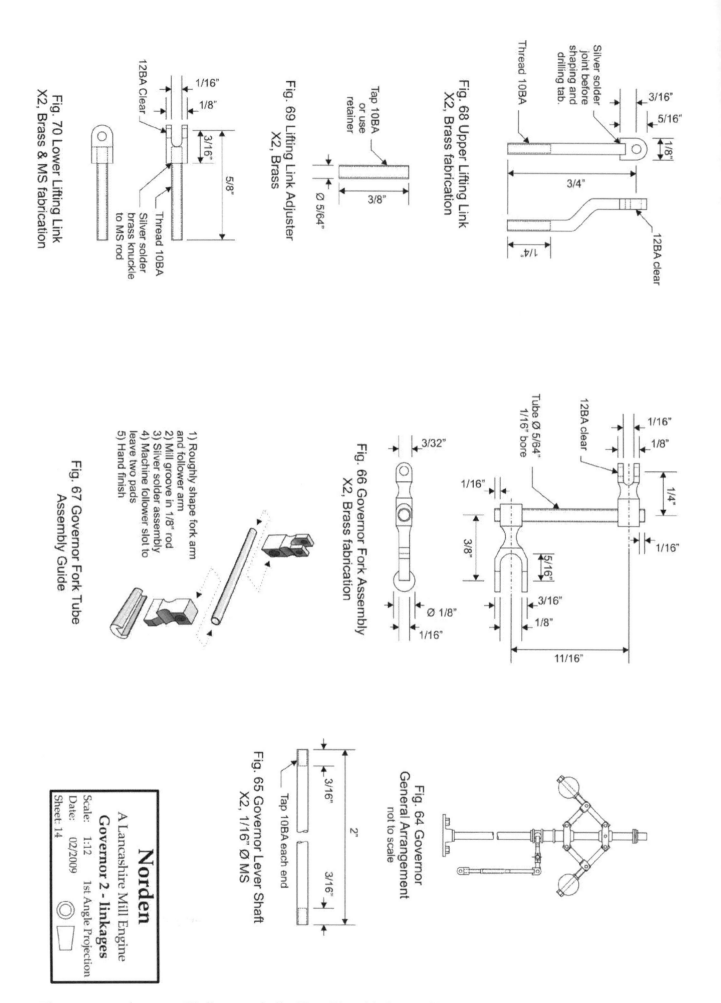

Fig. 70 Lower Lifting Link
X2, Brass & MS fabrication

12BA Clear

1/16"
1/8"

3/16"

5/8"

Thread 10BA

Silver solder
brass knuckle
to MS rod

Fig. 69 Lifting Link Adjuster
X2, Brass

Tap 10BA
or use
retainer

Ø 5/64"

3/8"

Fig. 68 Upper Lifting Link
X2, Brass fabrication

Silver solder
joint before
shaping and
drilling tab.

Thread 10BA

3/16"
5/16"

1/8"

3/4"

12BA clear

1/4"

Fig. 67 Governor Fork Tube
Assembly Guide

1) Roughly shape fork arm
and follower arm
2) Mill groove in 1/8" rod
3) Silver solder assembly
4) Machine follower slot to
leave two pads
5) Hand finish

Fig. 66 Governor Fork Assembly
X2, Brass fabrication

3/32"

Tube Ø 5/64"
1/16" bore

12BA clear

1/16"
1/8"

1/16"

3/8"

5/16"

1/4"

1/16"

3/16"

1/8"

Ø 1/8"

1/16"

11/16"

Fig. 65 Governor Lever Shaft
X2, 1/16" Ø MS

Tap 10BA each end

3/16"

2"

3/16"

Fig. 64 Governor
General Arrangement
not to scale

Norden
A Lancashire Mill Engine
Governor 2 - linkages

Scale: 1:12
Date: 02/2009   1st Angle Projection
Sheet: 14

The governor has two 5" diameter balls (fig. 63). This is at odds with the drawing, which suggests that the governor has much smaller balls (about 3"). As the quoted figure appears to be a direct measurement and 3" would be unusually small for a Watt governor (but appropriate if a Pickering governor was fitted), the size of 5" was taken as read. When I found pictures of the Chadwick engine, it was clear that it has a robust governor with 5" or even 6" balls.

The governor balls were turned from 1/2" brass bar using a form tool (photo 55). I made the form tool from 1/8" gauge plate, drilling a hole with a letter Z drill (a 10.5mm or 13/32" drill will be pretty close to scale too). I used a taper reamer to relieve the back of the hole and then cut out the tool to shape 'around' the hole. I drilled the brass 1/16" for the 10BA stud before shaping the balls, but not all the way through. Drilling right through caused the balls to 'part off' prematurely (photo 56). It is then a simple task to open the hole right through the balls once they are finished.

As drawn the governor spindle appears have some sort of horizontal connection to the steam chest right at the level of the bedplate. This could be artistic licence, as this seems an odd place for the steam control linkage it to be. It may be that the linkage was broken or missing when the original was observed. I assumed a more conventional arrangement (fig. 64). A cross bar is shown half way up the legs, scaling to 1 1/2" wide. It is positioned suitably to support a cross-piece for the governor lever, so I have assumed that this is what it is. I schemed out as simple a linkage as possible: a tube pivots on a bar (fig. 65) between the two cross pieces, this has a fork on one side that engages a collar on the lower part of the governor (photo 57). On the other side a lever lifts a link rod that in turn moves a lever that closes a butterfly valve in a housing on the front of the steam chest.

The governor fork assembly is almost entirely hand work (fig. 66). Like the governor arms the various holes should be pre-drilled in brass stock, but they should be silver soldered to the tube before finishing. At the same time a short section of 1/8" diameter brass with a slot milled or filed in it should be silver soldered onto one fork to make the 'followers' (photo 58). Both ends can then be finished to shape with relative ease (fig. 67). This is much easier than trying to file the two round pads. The tube needs to be a very easy fit on the 1/16" lever shaft, and I found that running a 1/16" reamer through the tube after soldering helped ensure this.

The links and levers were fabricated from brass and steel (figs 68, 69, 70). 1/16" mild steel rod can just be threaded 10BA, and you can get 5/64" brass tube that will similarly just take an internal 10BA thread. The upper and lower links and their adjuster are made using such material. Aside from working slowly and carefully, the best advice I can offer for making the small joints and tabs is to do as much work as you can before separating them from the parent stock. The rather tenuous grip afforded by these incomplete threads is enough to allow the governor mechanism to be aligned, but a drop of retainer is essential to make sure they stay where they are put.

The various parts pivot on 12BA machine screws, this something of a cheat, but making fitted bolts at this size is a bit of a challenge! The key is to ensure that all the joints in the governor (and its associated links) are completely free without any binding. A little slop is not a bad thing, but try to avoid too much lost motion. With the dimensions given the full movement of the governor should move the lever on the butterfly valve through about 60 degrees.

The butterfly valve is based on a design by *Tubal Cain* for his estate pumping engine, Lady Stephanie, and will be described next.

Mr Lees' little drawing shows no details of steam or exhaust pipes. The raised band around the cylinder may represent a loop in the exhaust passage. As this is at the same level as the exhaust port it does not affect the likely position of the exhaust – half way up the cylinder (photo 59). It would be typical for the steam pipe to be bolted onto a pad on the steam chest or its cover, bearing in mind the need for a throttle valve close to the steam chest. There is no indication of the governor valve placement. As described earlier, the chosen arrangement is for the governor to operate a lever fixed at the level of the cross-piece shown in the drawing, and for this in turn to operate a butterfly valve attached to the steam chest via an adjustable drop link (photo 60). Such an arrangement would follow prototypical practice. To facilitate assembly and the operation of a throttle the valve needs to be on the upper part of the cover. The position of the governor spindle dictates that the steam pipe must turn to one side – the opposite one from the governor valve controls.

It is sensible to assume a steam valve, although its location would depend on how the engine was installed. Naturally this would be a safe distance from the governor but as close as is reasonable to the steam chest, so I chose to place it just outside the table. The chosen arrangement puts the valve wheel about 2' (scale size) above floor level, low, but not too inconvenient for the engineer. A simple pipe could have represented the steam supply, but it's too late for that now. I started at the steamchest cover end, on which I had already made a 9/16" boss with four 10BA studs.

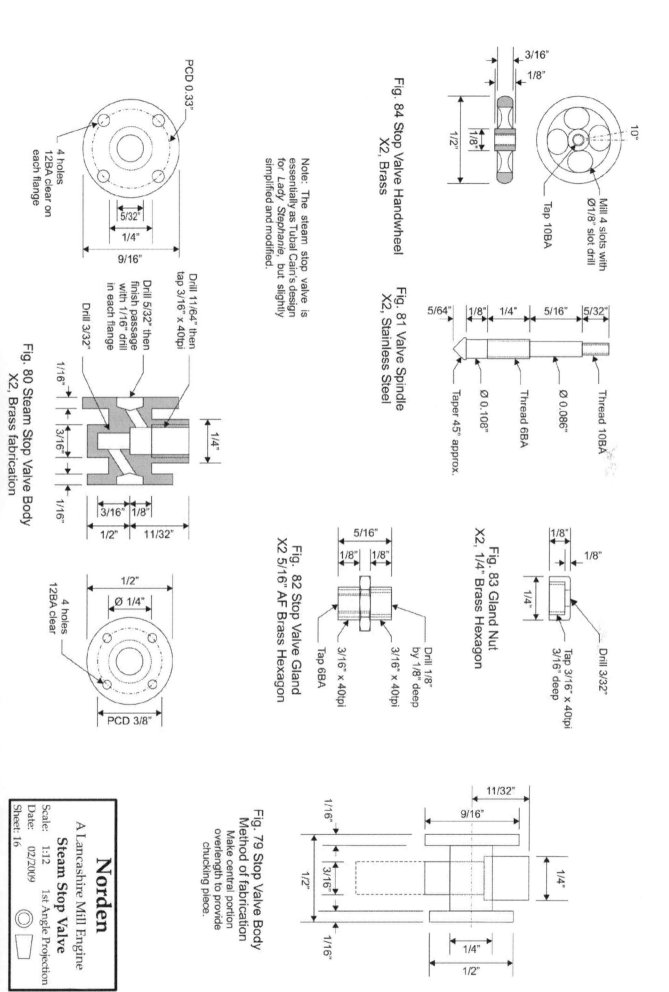

PCD 0.33"

4 holes
12BA clear on
each flange

5/32"
1/4"
9/16"

Note: The steam stop valve is essentially as Tubal Cain's design for *Lady Stephanie*, but slightly simplified and modified.

Fig. 84 Stop Valve Handwheel
X2, Brass

3/16"
1/8"
1/2"
1/8"
10°

Mill 4 slots with
Ø1/8" slot drill

Tap 10BA

Fig. 81 Valve Spindle
X2, Stainless Steel

5/64"
1/8"
1/4"
5/16"
5/32"

Taper 45° approx.

Ø 0.108"

Thread 6BA

Ø 0.086"

Thread 10BA

Drill 11/64" then
tap 3/16" x 40tpi
in each flange

Drill 5/32" then
finish passage
with 1/16" drill

Drill 3/32"

Fig. 80 Steam Stop Valve Body
X2, Brass fabrication

1/16"
3/16"
1/16"
1/4"

3/16"
1/8"
1/2"
11/32"

1/2"
Ø 1/4"

4 holes
12BA clear

PCD 3/8"

Fig. 82 Stop Valve Gland
X2 5/16" AF Brass Hexagon

5/16"
1/8"
1/8"

Tap 6BA

3/16" x 40tpi

3/16" x 40tpi

Drill 1/8"
by 1/8" deep

Fig. 83 Gland Nut
X2, 1/4" Brass Hexagon

1/8"
1/8"
1/4"

Tap 3/16" x 40tpi
3/16" deep

Drill 3/32"

Fig. 79 Stop Valve Body
Method of fabrication
Make central portion
overlength to provide
chucking piece.

11/32"
9/16"
1/16"
3/16"
1/2"
1/16"
1/4"
1/4"
1/2"

Norden
A Lancashire Mill Engine
Steam Stop Valve

Scale: 1:12
Date: 02/2009   1st Angle Projection
Sheet 16

For drilling the flanges make recessed and drilled disc templates from silver steel, hardened and tempered, as suggested by Tubal Cain (photos 61). These have the advantage that they allow the easy, accurate drilling of the flanges *after* they have been attached to the pipes. I have not drawn the pipes, as they are best fitted to suit the actual construction, but I have detailed the two sizes of flanges that are required (figs 77,78). I silver soldered the flanges just a little way from the end of the pipe, and carefully faced the ends – bearing in mind that the heat had left the copper very soft. Finally, I bent the pipes to fit. When fitting the flanges to each other, I suggest using a little smear of liquid gasket or similar to keep the joints steam tight.

The first fitting was the governor operated steam valve (photo 62). That for *Tubal Cain's* design for *Lady Stephanie*, an elegant beam engine, was an appropriate size and relatively straightforward to adapt. The valve body is fabricated from two pieces of brass bar, silver soldered together (fig. 71). This design uses an angled slice of bar as a butterfly valve, fitted in a slotted stainless steel spindle (fig. 72). This should be made from 1/16" bar. I slotted mine at on end using a thin cut-off wheel in a mini tool, and threaded it 16 BA at the other. This slotting operation is difficult and took me a few tries. If you can jig up some way of doing this under control, such as mounting.

The butterfly itself is just a tin slice cut from brass rod, in order to produce the elliptical shape and bevelled ends (fig. 74). Again this is quite challenging and it is perhaps easiest to make it over-thickness then temporarily secure it to a block with double sided tape or superglue so that it can be tidied up with a file.

The gland (fig. 73) can be turned up from 1/4" brass hexagon, taking care to keep thread and holes concentric. It is only decorative, as the valve needs to be very free in its action, so if you intend to run your engine on steam, not air, put three or four shallow grooves in the pivot to create a simple 'labyrinth seal'. The valve lever is best made by drilling the two holes first, and then cutting and filing the outer shape (fig. 75). Set the drop link from the governor so that it moves the lever either side of horizontal, with the valve being fully closed when the governor balls are at their maximum extent. Note that when the valve closes, it should hopefully stop the balls rising further and hitting the legs of the table. You could include a cross pin as a stop to keep the balls from rising too far. If you are willing to sacrifice the governor action to stop wisps of steam, another option is putting a very tiny o-ring in the gland (you can salvage these from discarded cigarette lighters).

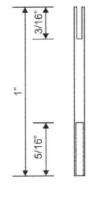

Fig. 71 Governor Valve Housing
X2, Brass Fabrication

1/16" 1/8" 1/16"
9/16"
Ø 1/4"
Ø3/16"
4 holes 10BA clear on each flange
PCD 0.33"
Thread 6BA and ream 1/16" after fabrication

3/16"
1"
5/16"

Fig. 72 Governor Valve Spindle
X2, Stainless Steel, Ø 1/16"

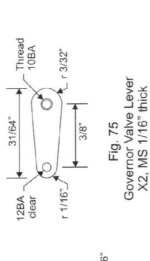

1/16"
1/4"
3/32"
3/16"
1/16"
3/16"
Thread 6BA

Fig. 73 Governor Valve Gland
Brass, 1 off

1/32"
3/16"
60°

Fig. 74 Valve Butterfly
X2, Slice of 3/16" Brass Bar

Thread 10BA
r 3/32"
31/64"
3/8"
12BA clear
r 1/16"

Fig. 75
Governor Valve Lever
X2, MS 1/16" thick

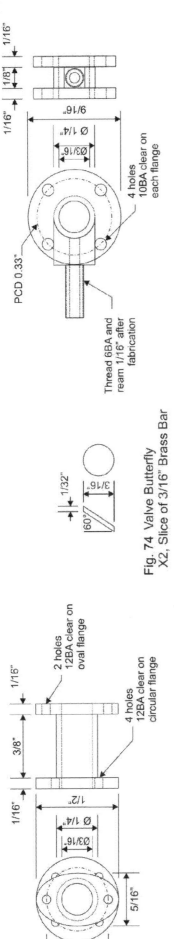

1/16"
3/8"
1/16"
1/2"
Ø 1/4"
Ø3/16"
2 holes 12BA clear on oval flange
4 holes 12BA clear on circular flange
5/16"
PCD 3/8"

Fig. 76 Exhaust Stub
X2, Brass

1/2"
Ø 1/4"
1/16"
4 holes 12BA clear
PCD 3/8"

Fig. 77 Pipe Flanges
X2, Brass, 4 off

9/16"
Ø 1/4"
1/16"
4 holes 10BA clear on one, 12BA on other
PCD 0.33"

Fig. 78 Pipe Flange
X2, Brass, 2 off

Pipework

The steam and exhaust pipes should be made from 1/4"Ø copper pipe.
The steam pipe needs to make a 90° bend to avoid the governor spindle.

The pipe flanges are best drilled after assembly to the pipes. Make drilling jigs by counterboring a socket for the flange in 1 slice of 3/4" steel bar, and drilling suitably positioned guide holes.

NOTE: The flanges for the governor valve and engine side of the steam stop valve are larger than the others.

Norden

A Lancashire Mill Engine
Pipes & Governor Valve
Scale: 1:12 1st Angle Projection
Date: 02/2009
Sheet: 15

In order to avoid the governor spindle, the next section was a 3/16" OD pipe bent 90°. It also supports the steam cut-off valve at a point just beyond the table. This has 1/2" flanges at each end. At the steamchest end it shares the 10BA studs of the governor valve, but it has 12BA screws at the steam valve end.

The steam cut-off valve (photo 63) was also to a *Tubal Cain* design, and is a fairly complex little model in its own right. The body is again fabricated from two pieces of brass silver-soldered together (fig. 79). I made the 3/16" spigot over length to provide a chucking piece. The body has a reduced 7/16" flange at one end, but both ends use 12BA fixings. The chucking piece made drilling and tapping of the body easier (fig. 80), just as well as this needs to be done accurately.

The valve spindle (fig.81) also took considerable care. I made it so the tapped end was furthest from the chuck, reducing the size one section at a time. After parting off over-length I reversed it in the chuck to make the taper. Ideally this could be done with a collet chuck, but I don't have a small enough collet.

The stop valve gland (fig. 82) was from 5/16" brass hexagon. In order to get the thread close up to the central portion, after cutting the initial thread I reversed the die, as the back of a die usually has much less 'lead' than the front.

The gland nut (fig. 83) is from smaller 1/4" hex material. I have ground the tip off my bottoming tap to help with treading such small parts. I didn't use an o-ring to seal the gland, but you could do so, though if you do you may need to slightly shorten the thread on the gland itself.

The final component of the stop valve is the handle (fig. 84). After turning the blank I used a rotary table to make the holes into short slots, but if you don't have such a facility you can just drill four holes, or enlarge them with a small round file.

The final section of pipe has a flange at one and is plain at the other to facilitate the easy attachment of a flexible pipe for low-pressure air or steam. I think this looks much better than an over-scale and incongruous union fitting.

It is likely that the raised band around the cylinder would have been a passageway for the exhaust, presumably for helping keep the cylinder warm. I have seen this arrangement in old engravings. It is also possible, but less likely, that the band is decorative or intended to support cleading. In any case, it seemed logical to locate the exhaust half way up the cylinder, level with the band.

The raised band limits the space available for a flange fitting for the exhaust (fig. 76). The exhaust pipe external diameter is 1/4" (scaling to 3"), and a 1/2" diameter flange is appropriate. To deal with this I made a short adapter with an 1/2" flange at each end, but drilled with the four holes at each end rotated by 45° (photo 64). I then filed one end down to an elliptical flange with just two holes, and used this to attach the adapter by two 12BA studs.

The final section of pipework had a flange at one end and the other cut at 45°, as is common practice on models. From habit I painted the cut section red; it helps make clear that the model stops here but in reality the exhaust would have led outside or to local steam heating (I doubt that this relatively primitive engine would have had a condenser).

We are nearly there! I have described all of the parts of the engine. Next I will cover a few finishing touches.

Before painting the model, I made many trial assemblies to make sure everything worked and fitted properly (photo 65). I won't go into great detail about how I painted the model. I used acrylic-based sprays, using a brown primer on the bare metal and finishing with deep green and black. These colours are modest and practical and well suited to a working engine. I made a small 'spray booth' from a cardboard box and tried to use many light coats (the table had over thirteen coats of green paint on it). The biggest two problems were how to spray parts all round in one go – I should have used some sort of turntable. The other was poor finish such as 'orange peel' or a matt finish. I understand these may be caused by spraying either too close, or in damp conditions respectively. The smallest parts, such as the governor were brush painted.

This is not a 'gold medal' finish, though it may be better than that on the original engine! In man of the photos a layer of oil doesn't help show off the finish either, but I'm more interested in 'watching the wheels go round' than watching the paint dry! Still I learned a few things and hopefully my painting skills are slowly improving (photo 66).

Mr Lees does not say anything about the makers of the engine, or their maker's plate, but as the maker of the model I claimed the right to mount my own plate on the engine.

Designs for the plate were produced in Corel Draw. A complex design with curved text was rejected as appearing too fussy, and three words in a simple ellipse were chosen to give maker's name, place and date. Two circles for mounting bosses were added just inside each end of the ellipse. The hardest task was choosing a suitable font; historically most plates used bold, tall sans-serif fonts. I don't recall which font I chose, but it was about as simple and clean as you can get.

For printed circuits, I use photo-sensitive boards that are exposed to ultra-violet light using a positive mask. The resist is developed using sodium hydroxide. It is possible to obtain spray-on photo resist for making your own boards, and this can be successfully used on brass. I have since had good results this way, but at the time I did not have any spray on photo-resist. Instead I followed another procedure that has been described in ME for making printed circuit boards.

This requires printing a mirror image version of the design on a laser printer – or photocopying a master copy. This is then 'ironed on' to a piece of 16-gauge brass with a very hot iron. Though it sounds simple, this process took three attempts. Vital to success was the use of masking tape to stop the paper slipping. I pre-heated the brass, stuck down the paper, then left the iron (on 'linen' setting) in place until the paper started to brown. Rather than peeling off the paper, I soaked it in water and gently rubbed it off to leave a positive area of 'resist' behind (photo 67).

The back, edges and unused areas of the brass were painted over and the plate etched in ferric chloride (as supplied for etching printed circuit boards). The solution was getting a little 'tired' and it took over three hours to get a good depth of etch; fresh solution would have been a lot quicker. A little heat would have helped as well. After filing the plate to size the background was filled with black enamel. When dry the raised letters were polished clean and the plate drilled then lacquered.

I made two false 'rivets' by Mounting 12BA hex screws in a mini-drill chuck and rounding the heads against an abrasive sheet. To fix the plate, these were glued into blind holes with cyanoacrylate (photo 71).

The bedplate of the original engine is, in its turn, 'bolted to a slab of concrete'. I decided to make a scale slab within a low retaining wall, and mount this on a wooden base. The wooden base is similar to a picture frame, from four pieces of beech. These were scavenged from old kitchen units and profiled using a router. The top was recessed to take a slightly inset rectangle of plywood. The beech looked rather 'contemporary' so I stained it a more antique looking dark oak with wood dye, then varnished it.

The (unstained and unvarnished) plywood was drilled for the six mounting 'studs' and rectangular plugs of balsa wood glued over the holes (photo 68) These prevented the 'concrete' blocking the holes. I then gave this central area a sizing coat of PVA ('white glue'). I was able to obtain a bag of fifty 1/12 scale frogged bricks; fortunately it actually contained 57 which was one more than I needed! These were the final stock of a long-standing ME advertiser, but I have since discovered that similar bricks can be obtained over the internet. To buy the quantities needed for a decent sized construction is quite expensive. In the early 1990s Stan Bray described a way of making bricks from fireclay, though this appears a long, slow process. I have tried using Das clay with limited success. Has any ME reader discovered an economic and effective way to mass produce miniature bricks? Some of the little handmade bricks had a ridge along one or more edges; these were removed by rubbing back and forth on a carbide grit file. This had some cost for my fingertips, but worked well.

Now for the 'bricklaying' itself. I first armed myself with some general information on the bricklayers art. I used quick setting mortar, which has the additional advantage of having a very fine texture compared to traditional mortar. I put another coat of PVA down and laid the first layer of bricks while it was still wet. It was remarkably easy to put the bricks down with a very thin but regular layer of mortar (photo 69). My trowel was a thick, soft plastic picnic knife. I used the excess mortar to fill in much of the central void. A couple of hours later, the second course of bricks went down just as easily and I began to muse of building a whole engine-house of tiny bricks…

The next day I drilled through the balsa plugs and trimmed them off level with the top of the bricks. I was now ready to fit the cast base in place. To make scale coarse concrete I needed some fine aggregate. I had bought a bag of aquarium gravel, but this scaled to pebbles of a couple of inches across. Chicken grit was the right size, but was pure oyster shell and didn't look right. A third try was bird grit - a nice mixture of tiny fragments of flint, crushed shell and limestone, with a tiny proportion of charcoal. Scaling as a coarse gravel, very much like the old, coarse concrete of many Victorian concrete. One or two larger pieces of shell had to be picked off the surface by hand but the end result was absolutely perfect.

This mixture was used to fill top off the void in the brick rectangle, the base was carefully fixed in place with 6BA studs. Finally, a final skim of concrete was added around the edges to bed everything in place. Having laid the bricks frog uppermost, there was also a good mechanical key for the edge of the concrete. Naturally a little attention with tissue and sponge was needed to tidy everything up.

A day later I everything was set and dry, but there was a white bloom of lime over the concrete. I lightly scrubbed this off with a 'kitchen scratchie'' and when dry it had a more mellow colour. I'm looking at it as I write this, and I must say that making the base has probably been as rewarding as making any of the moving parts (photo 70).

After looking at the completed model for a few years, I decided the rough 'concrete' was not to my taste, and 'tiled' the top of the base with miniature sandstone flags (photo 72).

Running the Engine

Setting the valves is always a critical task to get the best out of any steam engine, especially a small one like this. The first step is to adjust the length of the valve rod so that the valve travel is symmetrical, exposing the same amount of steam ports at either end of its travel. This is easiest to do, albeit rather fiddly because of the small size, with the steam chest cover removed.

The next task is normally setting the angle of advance of the eccentric. If you refer back to the section on the crankshaft, you will see that, because of the unusual method of construction instead of setting the eccentric, I experimented with different positions of the crank, holding it in place with superglue. I suggest finding a position where the engine will run and just using this until it is run in. Once you are happy the engine is running freely, you can experiment to find the best crank position for smooth, slow running and then fix it in place as detailed earlier.

I found that it was necessary to put a reasonable amount of effort into setting up and running in the engine. The issue was the arrangement of the guide bars, which were very sensitive to any unevenness in their mounting faces, especially after painting the model. Any tendency to misalignment caused binding that was fatal to the slow running that this engine is suited to. It may be that a period of faster running in will help, but if you do this it is a good idea to remove the governor, or restrain the balls from flying out so they don't hit the legs of the table.

The valve design for this engine is such that it will use minimal expansive working, and it should be happy on either compressed air or low pressure 'wet' steam. Mine runs happily on just 1.4psi of air, or the merest breath of steam. I have only run it for short periods on steam – just enough to prove the point. I put some steam oil in the steam line, most of which rapidly exited through the exhaust! For extended running a simple displacement lubricator would be ideal.

This is not an engine I would expect to be put to practical use, although powered by a few psi of steam I am sure it would happily run some scale overhead shafting and perhaps a selection of machine tools – such as the Stuart lathe and pillar drill.

Conclusion

All in all, building *Norden* was a very rewarding task. I learnt that it is worth consigning things to the scrap box, even if they are machined correctly, if they don't look right. One side effect of this was that I found I had about 50% of the parts for a freelance horizontal mill engine, based on one at Abbey Pumping Station in Leicester, in my scrapbox. Cylinder, steamchest and cover, piston and rod, eccentric. I also have most parts for a governor – the Abbey engine has none. Following through this exercise encouraged me to believe that even those bigger, more complex projects that I have pondered are achievable in time. Finally, it has also taught me a few things about realism, and convinced me that it is worth making an effort to make sure that even 'freelance' designs are proportionate to full size.

I am a regular user of the *Model Engineer* website forums, so if you have any questions or thoughts on this engine, please post them there. Even if you don't decide to follow suit, I hope you have found the story of *Norden* an interesting one, and agree that my model is a credible recreation of the engine Mr Lees found 'rotting away' in a mill in Norden, near Rochdale.

Castings now available for Norden

In the first chapter, I mentioned that I had sent the patterns for *Norden* to Blackgates Engineering. I received a set of sample castings from the patterns. Following an initial inspection, I had to put them to one side for a while as my lathe was out of action, in the process of being converted to variable frequency drive. A few other interruptions including a holiday held things up, but I have now been able to give them some proper attention.

The full set of castings supplied by Blackgates includes the following parts:

- Bedplate
- Cylinder
- Cylinder top cover
- Valve chest
- Valve chest cover
- Flywheel
- Large pulley
- Small pulley
- Eccentric strap

All of these castings are in cast iron, except the eccentric strap, which is gunmetal. This last casting is actually a *Tich* casting, but it is ideal for *Norden's* strap.

To keep the price of the castings reasonable, all the castings are made in a single mould and pour. This does make the casting of the very fine detail of the flywheel and pulleys with their very fine spokes a demanding task. These three castings did have a fair amount of flash on the spokes, but as the quality of the cast iron is very good it was surprisingly straightforward to tidy up the spokes.

I first tackled the small pulley, expecting the very narrow spokes to be badly chilled, however, the casting was readily worked with a small file. It took me less than ten minutes to file any extra metal back to the spokes.

The flywheel was a little more demanding. I had added a fillet to the right angles of the cross-shaped spokes, to help with releasing from the mould. Even so some moulding sand had clearly adhered to the pattern and partly filled the recess on several spokes. Unlike my original flywheel casting, which had chilled spokes, I found it surprisingly easy to remove this extra material using a 'pine tree' shaped diamond burr in a rotary tool. My technique was to angle the burr along the length of the groove in the spoke, and draw it along. It took twenty to thirty minutes to clean up the casting.

I completed machining the flywheel casting, aside for the keyway, although I made the bore 5/16", as I will be using it on a different model. This was an opportunity to use my new 100mm 3-jaw chuck. Again the casting machined freely, with no sign of chilling on the rim. I found that the dimple in the hub was slightly off-centre when I came to bore the flywheel. I solved this by using an FC3 endmill (any centre-cutting slot drill or end mill will do) in the tailstock chuck to create a small, flat-bottomed recess to replace the dimple. I was then able to centre, drill and ream the bore without difficulty.

The rest of the castings, aside from the gunmetal eccentric strap, are of the same easily machined iron. As the other castings do not have the same intricate shapes as the spokes, they all appeared to need minimal fettling before machining. The only thing to watch is that the core hole in the cylinder is not perfectly central. This should not cause any issues as the cylinder is bored out, but make sure you centre the casting relative to its outer surface.

I understand that Blackgates can also supply drawn steel angle for the table (which will be much easier to jig together than my black steel angle), and they have also sourced a pair of brass gears suitable for the governor. I am sure these castings and extra parts will provide a good start to anyone wishing to build *Norden*.

A final thought to finish this addendum – I am now convinced that the engine was a John Chadwick engine. I have found pictures of a few different engines, none the same as *Norden*, but with many related features and it would not be out of place among them. For example, one A-framed engine lacks the 'table-top' and has the flywheel placed centrally. The 19th century advertisement I found on the web shows the sheer variety of engine arrangement produced by this company, although the designs appear somewhat later than *Norden*.

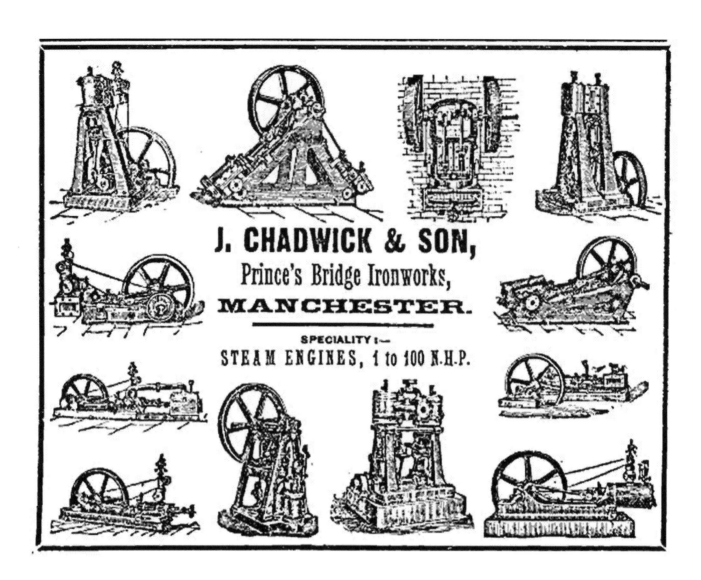

J. CHADWICK & SON,
Prince's Bridge Ironworks,
MANCHESTER.

SPECIALITY :—
STEAM ENGINES, 1 to 100 N.H.P.

Fin

Made in the USA
Middletown, DE
28 July 2021